# Honoring Christ in Caring for His Creation

## a second edition to "Christ & Creation"

Craig Sorley

Doorlight Publications
www.doorlightpublications.com

Published 2016 by Doorlight Publications

ISBN      0-9838653-4-5
ISBN-13   978-0-9838653-4-6


Cover Design:  Mike Gaudaur

**DOORLIGHT PUBLICATIONS**

This book is dedicated to my friend Simon Thomsett,
whom God used many years ago to open my eyes to the
environmental declines that we see in Africa today.
It is also dedicated to a growing number of fellow
Christians who are championing this cause
and who are helping others to recognize
our profound responsibility to
care for God's creation.

# ACKNOWLEDGEMENTS

I would like to gratefully acknowledge a collection of individuals who provided assistance in the development and review of this book. Their comments and suggestions improved both the substance and quality of the text. Special appreciation is extended to Tim Bannister (Farming God's Way collaborator) and John Elwood (USA board member), for their comprehensive reviews and insightful comments; for Pastor Erik Hyatt (New City Church), and his kind scrutiny and guiding suggestions in relation to theological matters; and to Pastor Benson Irungu (Membley Baptist Church), for his enthusiastic endorsement of this book as a Kenyan leader promoting a creation-care vision within his church here in Nairobi. I am also grateful to Chip Carter and Phil Manning (Rift Valley Academy), for their thorough attention to detail, corrections, and thoughtful comments. Appreciation is also extended to Michael Masso (missionary colleague at Moffat Bible College), who poured over the text and offered helpful insights. My family members (David and Darlene Sorley) and partners in ministry, including both Ed Brown and Antony Muga, also provided encouragement and suggestions for improvement.

Special recognition is also given to Mike Gaudaur (former teacher at Rift Valley Academy), for his creative efforts in designing the cover.

Finally, I want to express my heartfelt thanks to my greatest advocate, my wonderful wife Tracy, for all the support she provided, and my indebtedness to other members of the Care of Creation Kenya team as well, especially for their patience as I took time away from other activities to complete this book.

# CONTENTS

# Part 1
## My Journey Towards a Passion for Creation Care

# Part 2
## Our Savior's Creation Groans

# Part 3
# Biblical Principles Encouraging Us to Honor Christ in Caring for His Creation

# PART ONE

# My Journey towards a Passion for Creation Care

# Cancer, God, and a
# Newfound Conviction

I n 1989, as a 21 year old halfway through my second year of college, I laid in the hospital, fresh out of surgery, wondering how the next chapters in my life would unfold. Just a few days earlier a CT scan had revealed that I was suffering from a brain tumor. Nothing could have been more disconcerting to a young man, with all the hopes and dreams of life before him, to be suddenly entertaining the reality that life could be over in a few short months.

In the years prior to this momentous event, I had been privileged to spend most of my life growing up in East Africa, living for a number of years in Ethiopia, Uganda, and Kenya. My parents served as medical missionaries, and from an early age I was surrounded by men and women from the mission community who were working to advance the gospel of Christ in these countries. Within the context of this setting I grew to love the people of Africa, their food, and the beautiful landscapes and unique wildlife that God bestowed upon this continent.

As a teenager living in Uganda there were some important lessons that I learned from observing my father, who worked in rural villages training people in the area of community-based health care. The first was that God loves the whole person, and in the same way He wants us to express Christ's love for the whole person, both spiritually and physically. Focusing only on the spiritual needs of people, or only on their physical needs, is an incomplete expression of the gospel.

The second lesson I began to understand related to the most appropriate ways to help people with their problems. For example, in the case of a rural community lacking adequate medical care, it is often more beneficial and much less costly to train those communities in the prevention of illness. Setting up medical clinics can indeed be very beneficial and important, but supporting such clinics over time often requires funding from the outside, making them unsustainable. If no training in basic health care principles accompanies the effort, people must continually return to the clinic to be treated for the same illnesses that could easily be prevented.

These lessons reinforced the fact that in a place like Africa we need to redouble our efforts in equipping and training people to prevent or solve their own problems with their own resources. The essence of true "development" is linked to the "development" of people, and this is where the greatest needs lie. Long-term solutions are required for chronic problems, and when people grow in their ability to solve those problems it brings blessings that go far beyond the mere handouts of food and medicine that are often distributed during times of crisis, and which normally create dependencies as well. Early on I came to appreciate the wisdom of a well known proverb: "An ounce of prevention is worth a pound of cure."

When the AIDS epidemic began to emerge in Uganda in the early 1980's, the truth of this proverb could not have been more relevant. From a purely medical and physical standpoint, AIDS was totally preventable, yet the epidemic soon mushroomed across the country. Many years prior to this epidemic the Rev. Billy Graham had visited Uganda, expressing his admiration that it was one of the most Christian nations in Africa. Unfortunately, Christianity seemed to have little impact in preventing the spread of this killer disease. The epidemic grew quickly, not because of medical or physical inadequacies, but because people lacked the spiritual and moral commitment to follow God's ways in terms of sexual behavior.

As a teenager watching the emergence of the AIDS crisis I began to recognize how a spiritual commitment to God held tremendous implications for transforming the physical realities of life. My parents, and their fellow missionaries, fervently upheld the truth that a solid commitment to Christ provided the most promising solution to AIDS. A community dedicated to following the precepts and commands of our Lord could eliminate this disease from their midst within one generation.

While this was taking place, and as I watched my parents and others developing a God-centered approach to address this issue, I also began to notice another even more sinister problem that was beginning to emerge. This new issue would affect not just individuals who had contracted a disease; it would affect entire communities, landscapes, and regions. It would undermine the very life support systems that sustained those communities and their economies, adding yet another layer of hardship upon already difficult situations for many.

Growing up in Africa afforded me privileges that few boys from the West can enjoy. One of those privileges was the opportunity to witness, first hand, the glory and beauty of God as seen in the unique wildlife found on the continent. Being able to drive through a herd of elephants in a game park, fish for giant Nile Perch on the banks of the Nile where crocodiles lurked below, and watch lions creeping through the grass towards a zebra are all marvels that I wish every person could experience. The Africa that I knew as a young man was a wild and exciting place because I never knew what I might find around the next corner.

One special aspect of the breathtaking wildlife which caught my attention included the magnificent hawks and eagles of various kinds that seemed to be abundant almost everywhere I went. As my interest grew, I was fortunate to meet up with Mr. Simon Thomsett, East Africa's leading expert on birds of prey, who also introduced me to the sport of falconry. By this time our family had moved to Kenya and I was in my final year of high-school. My plans were to remain in the country for a number of months after graduation before returning to the US to start college. Through Simon I learned how to train, care for, and hunt with a hawk, and together we went on many excursions into unique and beautiful places. During these months I also began to learn more about the various environmental issues that were unfolding in this part of Africa. Little did I know how these experiences would shape my future as I entered the next chapter in my life, and this brings me back to the story of my cancer.

Upon returning to my home state of Minnesota to start college my passion for birds of prey remained with me, and I quickly joined the local falconry club. I learned how to enjoy God's creation in the out-of-doors, even in the midst of snowy winter months, as I trained and hunted with my red-tailed hawk along with other enthusiasts. Then the unusual headaches came to me in the middle of my sophomore year, where I had enrolled at what is now Bethel University, a Christian college and seminary.

I first noticed the headaches during November and December of 1988, but did not give them much consideration. Even though they persisted I went ahead and signed up for one of the short courses being offered during the interim session in January of 1989. This session took place between semesters, and I was very intrigued by one course in particular, on the topic of environmental stewardship, being taught by a biologist named Dr. Robert Kistler. The emphasis of the course was straightforward: as environmental concerns emerge around the world, Christians should respond appropriately to those concerns. Although the course was short, the issues that were raised resonated deeply from my own experience in Africa.

The headaches persisted, and a few short weeks after the course a CT scan revealed that I had a brain tumor. Immediate surgery was recommended by the neurosurgeon, and before my family could arrive back from Kenya to see me, I had been ushered into the operating room. The situation looked ominous, everything stopped in its tracks, and I knew I was about to face the darkest days of my life. To my surprise, and to the delight of my family, the surgery went well, and I woke up with all my fingers and toes still moving. This was good news initially, but some big unknowns now hung heavily in the air. What kind of cancer was this? Had it spread in small undetectable ways to other areas of my body? What was the prognosis for the future?

As it turned out, answering these questions would take time. We had to wait for more than two days to receive a report from the pathology lab. This waiting period was painfully long and difficult, knowing full well that death within a few short months could be lurking right around the corner. My heart was filled with fear as I tossed and turned during those prolonged and often sleepless hours. Then, very unexpectedly, on that final day, just hours before we were to receive the lab report and meet with the neurosurgeon, something took place that transformed my life forever. A reminder of my deep admiration for the wildlife of Africa, and my particular interest in hawks and eagles sets the stage for the significance of this event.

That morning I had decided to spend a few minutes flipping through a booklet filled with Scriptures as I waited together with family members for our meeting with the neurosurgeon. Given the circumstances, I was fearful and nervous, I was searching for comfort, and I was completely unprepared for how God was about to meet my needs in a most astonishing way. The very first (yes, the very first) passage of Scripture that I paused to read that morning was the one that follows:

> *"Praise the Lord, O my soul; all my inmost being, praise his holy name. Praise the Lord, O my soul, and forget not all his benefits - who forgives your sins and heals your diseases, who redeems your life from the pit and crowns you with love and compassion, who satisfies your desires with good things so that your youth is renewed like the eagle's." (Psalm 103:1-5).*

Within minutes of reading these words the most remarkable thing happened. My mind went back to Africa and I recalled the power and strength of the Crowned Eagle, the Martial Eagle, the Verreaux's Eagle, and other majestic birds. As I reviewed these memories the fear that had gripped my heart for several days melted away, the darkness faded, and a resolute sense of peace fell over me that I had never experienced before. There I was, a young man who was a sinner, a young man who was afflicted with disease, a young man who longed to be rescued from the pit of despair, and who desperately wanted his youth to be renewed like the eagle's. What greater comfort could I have requested? What more evidence of God's reality did I need? He was right there, speaking to me in my darkest hour, describing the very details of the depressing situation that I faced, and He was communicating a message of hope. As I pondered that final phrase, "so that your youth is renewed like the eagle's", I knew I had just experienced a most intimate moment with my heavenly Father. He had just validated, beyond all shadow of a doubt, the reality of His presence and the personal nature of His message.

My life was transformed that day. Even though the lab report and the visit from the surgeon that afternoon held out the possibility of tough times ahead, I had peace and confidence that God would bring me through them. And indeed that is exactly what He did. Although this was a dangerous cancer with a reputation for recurring, a cancer which required chemotherapy, radiation treatments and many months of recovery, I have now been cancer free for more than 27 years.

How did this event change my life? There were two main outcomes. The first was a transformation in my relationship with Christ. Years prior to this experience I had accepted Him as Lord and Savior, but unfortunately my passions had remained lukewarm. My commitments had been weak and I had been half-hearted in my walk with the Lord. Like never before, I now understood the unmistakable reality of the Christian faith. God is real. The truth of His written word is real. To skim over the surface of these realities was unwise. I could no longer treat them lightly. I could no longer be half-hearted in these matters. As a result I began to relish and enjoy my walk with Christ in a fresh new way, and I recognized that He wanted me to learn, grow, and to be changed more and more into His likeness. As never before, I came to the realization that a stagnant Christian is a very unfortunate contradiction.

The second result of this event goes back to the course I had taken at Bethel University, my friendship with Simon, and my years growing up in Africa. While I was still in the hospital, during those days following the report from the surgeon, I had a very clear sense that God had *"redeemed my life from the pit"* for a reason. As bad as this traumatic experience seemed at the time, God had something good in mind, even though He had to go to such extremes to get my attention. I knew very clearly that God was going to bless me by renewing my youth like the eagle. I had a calling to undertake and a task to pursue. That calling had already been planted into my heart, and it was about to germinate. It revolved around one simple question:

> *"How does God want Christians to respond to the growing problems that are affecting His creation?"*

9

With this question in mind, I began a new journey in life, which eventually led to the writing of this book. After completing several months of chemotherapy and radiation treatments, I began to regain my strength, and I made a return trip to Kenya for a time of rest and recuperation. It was here that I had a chance to be with family, to regain the weight I had lost, and to spend more time with my friend Simon. And it was here that the question above came into clear focus.

Together Simon and I spent long hours reflecting on the beauty and wonder of Africa, its landscapes, its birds and wildlife, its rivers and forests, the lakes and fish of the Rift Valley, and how that beauty and diversity was essential to the well-being of Africa's people. Unfortunately, we also grieved over the fact that this beauty was fading, and it was fading fast. What struck me most deeply one day was a question that Simon posed. "What are Christians doing about these issues? They don't seem to care at all about what is happening to the environment!" Little did Simon know how God would use that question to strengthen and confirm the calling I had sensed several months ago in the days following my surgery. It fanned the fire that had already been lit within my heart, leading to a conviction that would direct the course of my life.

After my visit to Kenya I returned to Minnesota, where I completed an undergraduate degree in Environmental Science and a Masters in Forestry with an emphasis in education. It was during this time that I began a determined search of what Christians were saying on this topic. Over the course of several years during the early 1990's I was to discover that Simon's allegation was right on target. When I would make comments about environmental issues or communicate my concern about creation, people in the churches I attended would give me strange looks. I quickly learned that for the most part, Christians had very little to say on this topic. It was like a blank page in their minds. I found that even most of the pastors and seminary-trained individuals had great difficulty in describing or articulating a meaningful biblical perspective related to creation care. While the church has definitely made some good progress on this issue in the 27 years since my experience with cancer, it is still a very new issue for most of us. Relatively few Christian books have been written on creation care. I have about 25 of them which I have collected over the years and they all fit comfortably on fifteen inches of my bookshelf.

The main point of this story is that Christians have neglected this dimension of life for too long, and it is time to give it serious attention. God transformed my life in a matter of a few days, and my prayer is that God will hasten the transformation that has already begun within the Church in how it responds to a groaning creation.

As the years have passed since these events and from my first-hand experience here in East Africa during the start of the 21st century, something has become remarkably clear to me. In many ways what is happening to God's creation is just like cancer. To some of us it may seem that we are only experiencing headaches, but we had better be careful. Some headaches, if not properly diagnosed, can be fatal. Merely prescribing aspirin or pain medication will not solve the problem. Much more rigorous intervention is required.

To recall a lesson from my youth, and to apply it to the context of creation care, "an ounce of prevention" is worth far more than a "pound of cure." It is worth multiple pounds of cure. In the case of chronic hunger and poverty, for example, we must no longer be content with simply handing out relief supplies when drought, famine, or other similar crises strike. At the very least we must double, if not triple, the efforts that we make to prevent these crises from happening in the first place.

Neither should we cast an unconcerned eye upon deforestation, overgrazing, pollution, the disappearance of wildlife, and other similar issues that undermine conditions for future generations. The declines taking place in these areas only bring insult to the one who created such remarkable wonders. Whether we live in a rural area of Africa, or in a big city in America, God has called Christians to pursue excellence in everything we do, and that includes being good stewards of His creation.

The unfortunate reality is that most of us within the Church are poorly equipped to think, talk, teach, preach or behave in a way that reflects a biblical worldview of creation. In the same way that a commitment to Christ holds the most promising answer to the physical scourge of AIDS, our commitment to glorify God on this topic holds tremendous implications for the physical health of landscapes around the world, and the people whose lives are sustained by those landscapes. If we ignore this topic, or give it less attention than it deserves, we compromise our witness as followers of Christ, and we commit the error of portraying an incomplete expression of the gospel.

Please join me, if you will, in striving to honor Christ and to love our fellow man, by caring for the creation our Lord has made.  May this conviction which God placed in my heart become a conviction within your heart, and may the Light of the world help us to see this issue through His eyes and from His perspective.  What Martin Luther expressed many years ago points us in the right direction.

> *"Now if I believe in God's Son and remember*
> *that He became a man, all creatures will appear*
> *a hundred times more beautiful to me than*
> *before.  Then I will properly appreciate the sun,*
> *the moon, the stars, trees, apples, as I reflect*
> *that He is Lord over all things."* [1]

*Martin Luther*

# PART TWO

# Our Savior's Creation Groans

# Headaches in Africa that are symptoms of cancer

## Introduction

As Africa enters the 21st Century we face a set of environmental concerns that are unprecedented in history. These include deforestation, the loss of biodiversity, land degradation and declines in per acre agricultural output, overgrazing, pollution, a warming and drying climate, and diminishing water supplies. All of these issues work together to perpetuate poverty, hunger, disease and death. What used to be occasional and infrequent difficulties have become chronic problems which affect millions of people each year. Christians must recognize that when our Savior's creation suffers from unnecessary abuse and neglect, people also suffer unnecessarily, and sometimes die as a result.

I will not give a lengthy discourse on each of these problems, but they deserve to be summarized for the sake of highlighting the urgency of the situation, and to provide the context necessary for the third and most important section of this book. When I found out about my cancer, I had to immediately reorient my entire life to fight a battle. Fortunately, with help from the Lord, and in ways beyond my own understanding, I was able to win that battle. It is my honest conviction that the Church must also reorient itself to fight a major battle, and we will need significant help from the Lord in the struggle.

As I write, keep in mind that I share a perspective that comes from a substantial amount of first-hand experience, personal study, and conversations held with a broad spectrum of people.  These people include local farmers, community leaders, scientists and friends, key African leaders, including personalities like the late Nobel Laureate Wangari Maathai, and long-term missionaries who have devoted their lives to serving the people of Africa for many years.

My intention is not to be an alarmist, or to exaggerate the facts, but to give an accurate description of the realities as I see them.  A diagnosis of cancer is a sobering thing, and I must be entirely honest in sharing that I am grieved by the serious nature of the facts below.  Before we get into the details, I also want us to keep in mind that these events are taking place in a region of the world where Christianity has expanded rapidly over the past five decades.

Below are some of the more serious headaches.  In the same way that a headache can be a symptom of something as life-threatening as a brain tumor, God's creation in Africa is exhibiting symptoms that threaten the current and future well-being of countless communities across the continent.

**Deforestation**
When we stop to consider the long list of benefits that trees and forests provide to mankind, we can begin to understand why God, out of everything that He created, chose the tree to serve as a symbol of life.  Across much of the tropics deforestation has been significant. Reports by the FAO and other scientific bodies estimate that about half of the Earth's

mature tropical forests have been destroyed since 1950.[2] This reality is quite evident across much of Africa, where the continent happens to boast one of the fastest rates of deforestation, sometimes twice as fast as seen in other parts of the world.[3] As one example, a first ever report on the state of the environment produced by the Kenyan government, which came out in 2004, revealed that closed canopy forests used to cover almost 10 percent of the country. Today that figure is less than 1.5 percent. In just a 30 year time span, from 1973 to 2003, it was estimated that Kenya had lost roughly 55 percent of its remaining woodland and forest cover.[4] This decline took place very quickly over the brief time span of just half a generation.

As a rapidly growing nation the demand in Kenya for timber, building materials and firewood is outstripping supplies. According to a 2015 report by the Green Africa Foundation, Kenya loses several million trees a day.[5] In a country of 48 million people, where about two thirds of the population use firewood and charcoal as a primary source of cooking fuel, this statistic is a realistic one. Isaac Kalua, the current chairman of this foundation, goes on to say that "Kenyans are replanting only 12 percent of the trees cut."[6]

Deforestation is affecting communities all across Africa. Each year finds women travelling longer and longer distances for ever dwindling sources of firewood. Just 20 kilometers from where I live, there is a community on the edge of the Rift Valley where many women spend long hours each week just collecting firewood and water for their families. The forest on this part of the escarpment was stripped years ago, and now women must trek into the valley itself to harvest wood from small trees in an area that is predominantly grassland. On a different part of the same escarpment, here in Kijabe, where I went to boarding school and currently work at Moffat Bible College, the story is very similar. More than 75% of the Cedar and African Olive forest that once carpeted this part of the escarpment in the 1980's has all been cleared. This has taken place in spite of trained government rangers who manage various outposts with the mandate to prevent illegal destruction. Today a private patrol of forest guards supported by local and outside donors is working to protect what remains of this forest.

While these examples are indeed unfortunate, what is most alarming in Kenya is the rapid deforestation taking place in the Mau Forest Complex. Comprising an area of roughly 400,000 hectares, this complex used to be celebrated as the largest remaining block of highland indigenous forest in East Africa. It serves as the country's most important watershed, providing rainfall that sustains 12 rivers and 5 lakes, bringing immeasurable benefits to thousands of agricultural communities in lower elevations. When it comes to tourism, both Lake Nakuru National Park and the Maasai Mara Game Reserve are blessed with important water bodies that depend entirely on the Mau forest. Together these protected areas bring more tourists to Kenya than any other parks in the nation. In the first 10 years after the turn of the century, from 2000 to 2010, 25% of the Mau forest had been destroyed.[7] Significant destruction has continued to take place since that time and it is uncertain where the total percentage of loss might stand today.

During two trips in 2015 I witnessed the grand scale of how this great forest is being destroyed. The soils under the Mau forest are deep and fertile. If managed properly this entire area could be a beautiful patchwork of farms in the valleys and forests on all the hillsides. It is a virtual goldmine that could provide healthy food, honey, and sustainably harvested wood products for decades to come, if it received proper care. Unfortunately the trees are coming down and the soils are being washed away, causing swollen rivers and flooding in low lying places like the town of Narok. A set of wonderful resources of great value are being wasted. In witnessing this tragedy I could only ponder with sadness how the continued destruction will alter the future, causing even greater hardship for the farmers and communities who are already struggling to make a living.

On a positive note:  Are there solutions to this headache?
Aggressive tree planting and reforestation efforts can be a very promising solution when planned and executed properly. There are a number of countries around the world where reforestation is a priority and where forest cover is actually increasing, including China, parts of Europe, and other nations in the northern hemisphere. While most deforestation takes place in the tropics, there are some countries in the southern hemisphere where the importance of healthy forest cover is gaining more attention. One ambitious example is the building of the Great Green Wall across the southern edge of the Sahara. Eleven countries have joined together with the goal of planting a belt of trees 15 kilometers wide and more than 7,000 kilometers long in an effort to protect arable land from encroaching desertification. Let us pray that this effort succeeds and that countries all across Africa will capture a vision for protecting and replanting forested areas.

## Soil Erosion, Agricultural Decline, & Hunger

Haile Selassie, the former Emperor of Ethiopia, understood the implications of erosion for his country. A story is told of how he was standing on the banks of the Nile, and as he witnessed the chocolate colored waters laden with soil he had tears in his eyes. He expressed his sorrow by commenting how the life of his country was flowing away to Egypt.

Here in Kenya years of poor farming practices combined with soil erosion have led to what many agronomists now describe as a soil fertility crisis.[8] Our soils can no longer produce what they used to. Even though agriculture is the backbone of the economy, providing employment to about two thirds of the population, and the raw materials for about two thirds of the nation's industries, relatively few farmers practice good soil conservation techniques. As a result, millions of tons of soil wash away from our landscapes. The actual loss in dollars is enormous, and some have estimated that each year, the value of lost soil is three to four times higher than the annual income earned from the nation's tourism sector.[9]

Poor soils stripped of their organic matter lead to poor harvests. Hundreds of small scale farmers I have interviewed over the years have all expressed discouragement over declining crop yields. Older farmers routinely report their yields are only 25-30 percent of what they used to harvest when they started farming back in the 1970's or 1980's. A study conducted by Roland Bunch across several African countries found that per hectare yields of staple foods have been dropping by about 5-10% per year (personal communication, February 6, 2016). This startling reality means that larger portions of land are needed to grow the same quantity of food. Unfortunately, due to a rapidly rising population, we have a shrinking land base here in Kenya, and obtaining additional land is not an option for most. A father with two hectares of good agricultural land must subdivide that land into smaller portions for his sons. In 1950, if you took into account the entire land mass of the nation, there were 9.6 hectares of land available for every Kenyan. By 2000 that figure had dropped to 1.9 hectares per person, and by 2050 it is projected to drop down to just 1/3rd of a hectare per person.[10]

Not only are we facing a land scarcity problem, but as coaxing food out of the ground becomes more difficult, the physical "poverty" resulting from declining crop yields is accompanied by an equally if not more serious problem. A "poverty of spirit" is taking root in our communities. As farmers wrestle with discouragement, a growing sense of despair and hopelessness is settling into their hearts. Unfortunately this "poverty of spirit" is being passed on to the next generation, and large numbers of young people across Africa are abandoning farming as a viable vocation. Many of our youth look upon farming as a bottom- of-the-barrel livelihood that is no longer profitable, and this holds serious implications for the future of agriculture. This reality can be seen in the demographic data which reports that the average small scale farmer in Africa today is more than 50 years old. If our farmers are growing older and our young people are abandoning farming, who will be growing our food in the future? Africa is already a hungry continent. A report by the UN's Food and Agricultural Organization (FAO) in 2015 reveals that 25% of the people in Sub-Saharan Africa do not have adequate amounts of food on a chronic basis, affecting some 200 million people.[11]

<u>On a positive note: Are there solutions to this headache?</u>
There are multiple solutions for arresting erosion and sustaining the fertility of agricultural land. Green manure cover crops using leguminous plants, for example, hold tremendous potential for restoring degraded soils. [12] Another encouraging solution is a movement now sweeping across Africa called "Farming God's Way". It has a proven track record to both heal degraded land and improve crop productivity at the same time. The real beauty of Farming God's Way is this: it is much more than just a new system of growing crops. It is a training program that stimulates farmers to capture a biblically-based vision for restoring their land and their soils. For more information see Appendix 3.

## Overgrazing

Large portions of the landscapes in East Africa happen to be grasslands that are not well suited to the growing of crops. As such, most of these areas are occupied by nomadic (or formerly nomadic) peoples who graze livestock for a living. In the past such cultures would move from place to place, feeding their animals and allowing grazed areas to recover in their absence. But as populations have grown, a man grazing his animals today will go over the hill to find that another man is already there with his animals. The result is a serious problem of overgrazing.

Art and Mary Ellen Davis are missionaries who have served in Kenya for more than 40 years. Their story highlights both how quickly our grasslands have changed and the extent of damage that has taken place.

*"We moved to Orus in East Pokot in January 1985. Everywhere we went the grass was waist high. You could not see rocks or holes in the ground and driving though this grass was a precarious business. Little did I realize that significant overgrazing would occur over the next twenty years. The Pokot were allowed by top officials to get AK 47s, with which they wiped out all the game, including all carnivores, and the herds of domestic livestock increased tremendously. Today the very land we walked on and drove over in 1985 is a semi desert wasteland with only scrub thorn bushes and bare, dusty and rocky ground. "*

I can tell a similar story right here in my own neighborhood of Kijabe, which is perched on the edge of the Rift Valley. Back in the 1980's we used to cross the valley in our journeys to Lake Naivasha to fish for black bass. In those days the grass was robust, healthy, and also waist high. Today there are thousands of goats, sheep and cattle that continuously graze the landscape year round, to the extent that the grass rarely grows taller than a couple of inches, even when this part of the valley is green from the rains. The process of desertification has already run its course and has scarred huge portions of what used to be rather abundant grasslands here in Kenya.

On a positive note:  Are there solutions to this headache?
Overstocking of animals on the worlds grazing lands is a challenging issue, especially when pastoral peoples have no clear regulatory policies or enforcement structures to carefully manage animal numbers. In the Old Testament, the flocks of Abraham and Lot were so large that Abraham wisely suggested the two families should part company. This was done to minimize tension between the herdsmen in these

families, who were competing for both water and grassland resources (Genesis 13).

Solutions do exist, such as rotational grazing and cut-and-carry systems that feed animals kept in enclosures. "Hope in a Changing Climate", a documentary by John D. Liu, is a remarkable story of environmental restoration in China. Goats were managed in a cut-and-carry system as one of several interventions that brought healing to the heavily overgrazed landscapes on the Loess Plateau. See the You-Tube video at: *www.youtube.com/watch?v=bLdNhZ6kAzo.*

## Decline of Water Supplies

The combination of deforestation, erosion and overgrazing has a sinister effect upon people by undermining available water resources. A question that is often raised by local communities here in Kenya is stated as follows: *"Why are we experiencing more droughts and more floods?"*

The obvious answer lies in the large-scale damage inflicted upon our watersheds, where landscapes are no longer able to capture and hold water in place when the rains arrive. Instead of soaking into the ground, much of the water that falls from the skies flows quickly off the land, resulting in varying degrees of runoff and flash floods that rob people of both water and soil. After the rains have ended the land dries out more quickly because it never had the chance to absorb much moisture in the first place.

The evidence of damage to our water supplies is now being felt across the country. I hear reports from local communities on a regular basis about previously permanent streams and rivers that have become seasonal or that have dried up altogether. These include even some significantly large rivers. In the living memory of local communities these rivers have always flowed with water, even in the midst of bad droughts, but today things have changed. Similar reports are also being given about wells and boreholes which serve as critical dry season water supplies. Without the protective carpet of forest, grass, and other vegetation that help to trap and absorb water, the rainfall intended to replenish our underground water supplies now escapes quickly, entering streams and rivers that flow into the Indian Ocean. On several occasions I have witnessed swollen and sometimes raging rivers where huge volumes of water disappear within a few short days, leaving behind communities that could have reaped multiple benefits from that water.

Close to home this has a direct impact upon both myself and my fellow Kenyans. One man tells the story of a stream on his family's land that now flows at a trickle compared to when he was a boy. His family used to dip water, as much as was needed, by plunging 20 liter buckets into this stream. Today it takes considerable time to fill a single bucket. In my own case I happen to enjoy some of the fishing opportunities that can be experienced here in Kenya. During a trip near the foothills of Mt. Kenya I stopped by the Naro Moru River Lodge, once a favorite location for trout fishermen. Today that river rises quickly after a rainfall, but afterwards the levels drop almost as quickly to a flow and depth so small that it no longer supports its former trout population.

<u>On a positive note: Are there solutions to this headache?</u>
Tree planting, the establishment of vegetated buffer zones along streams and rivers, erosion control measures, the installation of small dams, etc. have all been very effective in restoring the hydrological cycles of watersheds. As an encouraging example, take time to view the documentary from China, mentioned above in the section on overgrazing.

## Rainfall Patterns, Drought, and Climate Change

One of the grievances that I hear from Kenyan farmers on a regular basis relates to the erratic nature of today's rainfall patterns. I can verify their complaint because I have clearly witnessed the reality of this problem over the past 15 years. Rainfall that used to be predictable and consistent is now unpredictable and inconsistent. Since 98% of Kenya's crops are completely dependent upon rainfall, this has become a serious headache for many farmers.[13] Climate change is not something that will affect the poor in the future; it is affecting them today.

Clear examples of erratic rainfall problems have occurred quite regularly. Tempted by a few initial showers, farmers will often plant their seed only to watch the young crop germinate and die when additional rainfall does not arrive. In some cases the rains have started and stopped several times over the course of a few months, resulting in a situation where farmers have to plant their seed several times in a season. The reverse has also been true, when rains unexpectedly arrive during periods traditionally known as the dry season. In these cases farmers are caught off guard and they are unprepared to take advantage of the moisture in the soil. Do they run the risk of planting a crop now, which might fail, where they could lose their investment and look foolish in front of their peers? Or do they play it safe, hoping that good rains might come during the time traditionally known as the rainy season? With so much uncertainty the question of when to plant their seed has become a challenging guessing game for many farmers. With already meager resources at their disposal, this kind of situation is a discouraging prospect for those striving to raise food for their families.

Along with rainy seasons that are often diminished in amount, or which start too early, too late, or not at all, comes the growing frequency of serious drought. The reality of changing weather patterns is an issue that now receives regular attention and is discussed by communities almost everywhere I go. On the one hand it is true that a substantial part of this problem is directly related to all the damage that has been inflicted locally, through deforestation, erosion, and overgrazing. On the other hand something on a larger scale is also taking place. Continent-wide things are getting drier and this is a very real and urgent problem. You can see it in the landscapes just like you can see it in the face of a family member who has just walked through the door, and with one glance you know they are stressed out and not feeling well.

On a positive note: Are there solutions to this headache?
The encouraging news is that all the solutions described above will provide significant benefits to the problems we are experiencing with rainfall, drought, and our climate. Farming God's Way, for example, can be a very effective means of capturing and conserving water in our soils, equipping farmers

with one of the best tools to help them cope with the problems of drought. If implemented across landscapes on a country-wide scale by millions, these relatively simple solutions hold remarkable potential for effectively addressing most of our land degradation issues.

## Loss of Biodiversity

With the issues I have outlined above it is not difficult to understand the toll this has taken upon animal and bird populations. I rejoice in a God who ordained a place like Kenya to be rich in diversity, and at the same time I grieve as I watch how both plant and animal diversity are being lost.

When I first came to Kenya as a young boy in the mid 70's I can recall the gorgeous beaches and coral reefs on the coast. I spent hours snorkeling, and getting sunburned, as I enjoyed the vast array of colorful fish that seemed to be everywhere. Large and colorful shells of various kinds were abundant, and I confess I was one who collected many of them. Today when you visit the coast the fish are still there, but not in the teeming numbers of the past, and for the most part the shells are gone. In the same way many of the corals once so colorful are no longer thriving and have lost much of their former beauty.

Later on, as a teenager with a budding interest in birds of prey, I recall the long road trips our family would make back and forth from boarding school. During those journeys I used to count multiple species of these grand birds. Almost everywhere we went there was a hawk, a large eagle or a group of vultures gracing the skies. This was true even in the early 90s when I conducted some formal road counts of Kenyan raptors as part of my undergraduate program, where I recorded many species that were abundant.[14] Just 30 years later, when I look up into the skies today, I find them to be relatively empty. There are many species of hawks and eagles that I never see anymore. This is understandable since fewer nest sites are available due to deforestation, not to mention the fact that local communities are rather hostile to such birds as they sometimes prey on their chickens. A marked decline has also taken place in the populations of birds and the small mammals which serve as their food base. Of particular concern is the precipitous drop in vulture populations over the past 15 to 20 years. Some reports indicate that numbers have declined by 90% during this brief period, and today most vulture species in the country are endangered.[15] Predatory birds play an important role in our ecosystems. They also serve as important indicator species, and their presence is a good sign of a healthy ecosystem. Here in Kenya our birds of prey are vanishing.

A unique story related to bird life that I will never forget came from a missionary in Tanzania. She had been travelling across the country by bus, and during the periodic stops that took place at small towns along the way she was horrified when local people came forward with trays of roasted songbirds to sell as snacks to the passengers. For many years bird life of all species has been protected by law in countries like Kenya and Tanzania. Yet when hunger strikes, and when songbirds can be easily snared using mist nets or other traps, they become a ready source of food to eat or sell. In places where these practices occur, bird populations have suffered dramatically.

There are other unsettling facts that deserve to be mentioned regarding the well-being of our wildlife communities, and when you take the time to examine all the facts the list can grow long. From fish species that are extinct in Lake Victoria to many of our more glamorous large animals, we have reason to be concerned. I have noted a substantial drop in giraffe populations here in Kenya, and we are all aware of the unfortunate upsurge in the poaching of elephants and rhinos across Africa during the past five years. It is estimated that in 1900 Africa was home to four or five million elephants. Today the numbers are down to a figure of less than 400,000. In our national parks thousands of wire snares are found and removed each year, illustrating the pressures of the illegal bush-meat trade and the unlawful poaching that afflicts a wide range of wildlife species.

Perhaps most striking, however, is the poisoning of predators like lions, hyenas, and jackals. Just a last year, in late 2015, a very famous pride of lions right in the middle of Maasai Mara was poisoned by lacing a carcass with a lethal agricultural pesticide. In this case the Kenya Wildlife Service rushed to the scene with an antidote, and several lions were saved. Unfortunately, this kind of poisoning has occurred on numerous occasions, often in remote locations that go undetected, and when this happens many other predators that come in to feed on the leftovers can also be poisoned. Elephant poachers have often resorted to the same tactic. Guns are loud but poison is a silent killer, and with fewer vultures in the sky it is becoming more difficult for rangers to pinpoint where poaching activity is taking place. Today lion and cheetah populations across Africa are only a fraction of what they used to be. About 50 years ago it was estimated that 200,000 lions existed in Africa. Today the numbers hover around 20-25,000.[16] Here in Kenya, at the turn of the century, we had about 15,000 lions in the country, and today that number is less than 2,000.[17] One of my favorite experiences in Africa is to fall asleep in a tent and listen to lions roaring in the distance. My own sons have had this opportunity on rare occasions, but I often wonder if my grandchildren will have the same opportunity.

The challenge facing our wildlife is highly unfortunate because in a place like Kenya tourism is one of the mainstays of the economy. People come from across the world to marvel at our lions, elephants and giraffes. They come to celebrate the many species of wildlife that grace this land. These are creatures that God created as a marvelous reflection of His beauty. These creatures also fulfill a critical role in supporting the livelihoods of people. In 2014 nearly 600,000 jobs were created by the tourism industry, and the sector as a whole earned the nation an estimated 87 billion shillings.[18]

On a positive note: Are there solutions to this headache?
In spite of enormous challenges there are some success stories to celebrate where people have found creative ways to live in harmony with wildlife. Here in Kenya many species would have disappeared long ago without the tourism industry, and Mountain gorillas may be extinct today without safe havens like Volcanoes National Park in Rwanda. One very notable example comes from Namibia, where the profits from wildlife conservancies are used to provide direct

benefits to local communities in the form of schools, daycare facilities, and clinics.[19] And just recently it was reported that tiger populations have actually increased in places like India and Russia.[20] These examples do provide hope. Let us pray that we can find better ways to protect and appreciate the unique value of God's creatures.

## Closing Remarks

What is most disturbing about the trends I have been describing is the speed at which they are taking place. Conditions here in Kenya are changing so fast, and many of us residing within the country do not realize how quickly this cancer is growing. Unfortunately, this is true of many countries around the globe. We have forgotten the fact that what is good for creation is also good for people. When the creation groans people groan, and this suffering often takes the form of increased poverty and hunger.

It is essential that we develop a God-centered response to the challenges of deforestation, soil erosion, overgrazing, and the impact they are having upon our water supplies and the rich diversity of life so essential to the health of our landscapes and economies. Such issues deserve our full and vigilant attention. But we must begin this endeavor at a most important starting point. Our vision and response to this crisis needs to be cultivated and grown out of a focus upon God, the exploration of His word, and from a sound commitment to honor Christ.

As we have seen, there are some encouraging examples worth celebrating, and solutions already exist to address most of these problems. Unfortunately, the success stories are few and far between, and the number of people who have a firm commitment to implement those solutions is far too small. A change of heart is needed on a global scale, and people from all walks of life need to get involved.

The roots of caring for God's creation go far deeper than a simple notion that it's the right thing to do. When properly examined, the Scriptures provide a wealth of teaching that can serve to convict the hearts of people, and a conviction from God can lead to the transformation of hearts and minds. A stronger relationship with Christ leads to meaningful behavior change, resulting in practical action that brings glory to the Creator.

As we shift gears to focus our attention on lessons from Scripture, let us recall a thoughtful insight from Lutheran scholar Joseph Sittler:

> *"When we turn the attention of the church to a definition of the Christian relationship with the natural world, we are not stepping away from grave and proper theological ideas; we are stepping right into the middle of them. There is a deeply rooted, genuinely Christian motivation for attention to God's creation, despite the fact that many church people consider ecology to be a secular concern. 'What does environmental preservation have to do with Jesus Christ and his church?' they ask. They could not be more shallow or more wrong."*[21]

PART THREE

# Biblical Principles Encouraging us to Honor Christ in Caring for His Creation

# Introduction

*"We know that the whole creation has been groaning as in the pains of childbirth right up to this present time."*
Romans 8:22

I hope that Part Two of this book has brought us into a clear understanding of the urgent situation at hand. Every dimension of our Savior's creation is groaning in serious pain and the description given in Romans 8:22 rings true. The relevance of this passage is becoming more prominent as time goes by. We do live in a fallen world polluted by the countless entanglements of sin. While this groaning is seen all across the globe, in Africa there are many places where circumstances on the ground are particularly acute.

My own conviction is that nothing less than a complete transformation of perspective and behavior is required. Those of us who adhere to the Christian faith must understand that we have something very powerful to offer. The kind of transformation that is required is readily accessible when we bring this issue to the foot of the cross. We should be leading the world by example in providing a robust and thoughtful response to a creation that groans.

As we will soon discover, Christ is not only the cornerstone of our faith, He is also the Creator of all things, and therefore, He is the most appropriate starting point when we consider creation. Since Christ exhorted us to love God wholeheartedly and to love our neighbors as ourselves, we have a divine obligation to honor the Creator in our treatment of what He has made. We have a profound responsibility to consider how our treatment of creation will impact other people, both now and into the future. Caring for creation, therefore, finds its firm foundation in the person and work of Christ.

Part Three of this book is about putting God back into His rightful place, at the very center of our perspective as we relate to creation. How we use and care for land, fish, forests, water and other resources all needs to flow from a determined commitment to glorify the One who originally created the wonders of this world.

In the principles that follow my goal is to continually point us back to the Scriptures, highlighting how the concept of creation care is something that can be drawn from many aspects of our faith and many truths that we uphold and cherish. My intention is not to answer the question of how we should care for creation, but to firmly establish the biblical and moral rationale of why we should give careful consideration to this topic.

Each principle will bring us back to the same conclusion, demonstrating how a vigorous commitment to care for creation fits into the very core of our Christian faith, and one by one we can join these principles together into a solid and unshakable foundation. The world today desperately cries out for sound Christian leadership on this topic, and with this foundation in hand we can make the world a better place as we keep in step with our goal to advance the cause of Christ.

Principle 1

# We care for creation because Christ our Savior is Christ the Creator

In my own journey of discovery I have already mentioned the challenges I faced in being guided and nurtured towards a God-centered worldview of creation. As a young man, hungry for a biblical perspective on the topic, I had to embark upon a deliberate search for truth that was not readily available in the Christian circles I associated with. A number of years were required to piece together a theological framework that I found to be thoroughly satisfying, and there is still more that I need to learn.

One aspect of this search revolved around a simple question. If we were to develop a theology of creation, if we were to build a biblical foundation supporting the argument that Christians should be excellent stewards of creation, what would be the critical, essential, and indispensable cornerstones of that foundation?  In my own view Colossians 1:16 and John 1:1-3 serve as some of the most important places to begin because they reveal a most fundamental and transforming truth.  Constructing a biblical worldview of creation and a God-honoring response to environmental issues must begin with keystone scriptures like these.

> *"He [Christ] is the image of the invisible God, the firstborn over all creation. For by him all things were created; things in heaven and on earth, visible and invisible....all things were created by him and for him."*
> *(Colossians 1:15-16)*

> *"In the beginning was the Word, and the Word was with God, and the Word was God. He was with God in the beginning. Through him all things were made; without him nothing was made that has been made."*
> *(John 1:1-3)*

The truth these passages reveal may appear to be simple at first because we are so familiar with them, but when examined thoughtfully they are stunning and profound in light of the topic at hand. If we were to ask *"Why should we care for creation?"* the first and most primary answer is the fact that Christ our Savior is Christ the Creator. The very Author of our salvation is the Author of creation. When unpacked, absorbed, and assimilated to its fullness, this reality serves as a most important cornerstone, and it opens up a whole new perspective that many Christians have not paused to consider.

We should care for creation not merely because it is a good idea, but because of the epic, magnificent, and overwhelming truth that we owe absolutely everything to the One who made it all. This Savior, this Creator, gave His very life for all of mankind. And for those of us who claim Him as Lord, He is the very centerpiece of our lives. He stands before us as our cherished, most beautiful, and most treasured possession. In the light of this truth the gross inconsistency of attitudes and behaviors that often inflict harm upon creation become glaringly obvious. We cannot claim to legitimately love our Savior while at the same time participating in the careless abuse or destruction of what He has created. We must recognize the unavoidable fact that when we tarnish Christ's creation, we tarnish the name of Christ.

The One whom we claim as Lord, whom we acknowledge as our ultimate authority, the One who is our Savior, who rescued us from certain death and the penalty of our sin, the One who is our sin conqueror, who helps us win battles of temptation because He too suffered and was tempted (Hebrews 2:18), the One who sustains our very lives each and every day (Hebrews 1:3), He is also the One who has created everything that we see around us. We are deeply indebted and deeply grateful for all that He has done. How then should we act in relation to His creation? We must do so in a way that honors Him.

If we pause and reflect on this concept, a simple analogy from our human experience drives the point home. This analogy was first brought to my attention by Ed Brown, the director of Care of Creation Inc., in his book entitled *"Our Father's World."*

For those of us who are parents we can all appreciate the delight we experience when our children come home from school, especially when they eagerly run up to us and say something like: "Mommy, Daddy, look what I made for you!" As we take what is often a simple piece of artwork into our hands, we respond with joyful enthusiasm, and we praise that little child for their progress and achievement. Even though that artwork has no economic value to speak of, we still place value upon it. We do not crush our child's spirit by crumpling up such items and throwing them into the trash, but rather, we post them on a door or wall in our home to display and celebrate his or her accomplishment.

How does this help us as we consider the reality that Christ is the author of creation? The reason that we post our child's artwork on the wall, and give significance to those simple pieces of paper is not because they have any kind of monetary value, but because we have a very special and precious relationship with the little person who drew them. We love that little boy or girl. This very same principle should apply directly to our worldview about creation. The first and most important reason why we care for creation is because we have a very special and precious relationship with the One who made it all, and we love Him! As Ed Brown puts it:

> "If I can place a high price on things that have little or no intrinsic value simply because they were made by one of my children, how much more ought I to value and care for this amazing world God made, this world that is precious because He made it and that represents an excellence and beauty far beyond anything that any of us could begin to comprehend, let alone make on our own."[22]

When we examine this analogy from a purely economic view, we can easily recognize that there is one key difference between our child's artwork and creation. What Christ has made embodies untold ecological and economic value that we can only begin to estimate. It is a continual life-producing and life-sustaining system. Trillions of dollars would represent but a mere shadow of the accumulated value that we receive from creation each year.

But for Christians there is an additional and far more significant value that we must consider first. That value is revealed at the very end of Colossians 1:16. If all things were created by Christ, what do those final two words mean when they say that all things were created "for him"? There is something critical here that needs to inform our perspective. What those final two words reveal is the ultimate purpose for which Christ made the creation. There is a primary and supreme reason why creation exists, which provides it with a value far beyond what we might assign in purely economic terms. The essence of creation's purpose, the essence of its inherent value, is that it was made to stand as a testimony of Christ's beauty. All things were created for His glory. A very well-known Christian leader named Jonathan Edwards once wrote a statement which supports this truth.

> "We have shown that the Son of God created the world for this very end, to communicate Himself in an image of His own Excellency.....When we behold the light and brightness of the sun, the golden edges of an evening cloud, or the beauteous rainbow, we behold the adumbrations of His glory and goodness, and in the blue sky, of His mildness and gentleness."[23]

This is what followers of Christ need to fully embrace: Apart from the Scriptures, the creation serves as our most complete and spectacular physical evidence of Christ's reality and splendor. The excellence of the Artist can be seen in His artwork. As Romans 1:20 states:

> "God's invisible qualities – His eternal power and divine nature – have been clearly seen, being understood from what has been made, so that men are without excuse."

43

There are a number of other passages from the Bible which point in this direction, with Psalm 19:1-4 being one of the more commanding examples when it proclaims the following:

> "The heavens declare the glory of God; the skies proclaim the work of his hands. Day after day they pour forth speech; night after night they display knowledge. There is no speech or language where their voice is not heard. Their voice goes out into all the earth, their words to the end of the world."

Similar to what Jonathan Edwards and Romans 1:20 have revealed, here we see that "creation" declares a powerful message on God's behalf. And it does so on a continual basis in a language that all peoples of the world can understand. Creation's value and purpose is centered upon this vital and enduring role that it plays in revealing God to the world of men. When we take this divine and spiritual value, appointed to creation by God Himself, and if we add it together with the ecological and economic value that creation holds for the physical benefit of mankind, we can then realize the unmistakable and supreme obligation that we have to care properly for what Christ has made. We can also realize that when our activities bring ruin or destruction to creation, we commit an offense by snuffing out something that was meant to bring glory and honor to our Lord.

So three things come together here that must be preeminent in our thinking. Christ is the cornerstone of our faith, He is the Creator of all things, and all things were created for a divine purpose – "for Him". These realities are essential to a biblical worldview about creation. And since Christ exhorted us to love our neighbor as ourselves, we must give careful regard to how our treatment of creation may affect others. Caring for creation, therefore, finds its firm foundation in the person and work of Christ.

Principle 2

# We care for creation because it is a means of fulfilling the Great Commandment

In Matthew 22:34-40 we read the interesting story of how the Pharisees, standing in opposition to Jesus, made an attempt to test him. They posed what they thought would be a difficult question by saying: *"Teacher, which is the greatest commandment in the Law?"* Jesus was not at all distressed by their challenge and gave the following answer:

> *"Love the Lord your God with all your heart and with all your soul and with all your mind. This is the first and greatest commandment. And the second is like it: Love your neighbor as yourself."*

If someone requested us to select a single passage from the Bible to describe what lies at the core of the Christian faith, many of us might legitimately turn to this passage. Around the world countless people recognize this statement by Christ, including those who adhere to different religions. God's word is like a double edged sword. It is so sharp and convicting that some passages are known worldwide.

While millions, even billions, are familiar with this timeless exhortation, few of us ever stop to ponder the totality of what God's word is saying. This is nothing less than a call to perfection, not just in certain areas of life, but in all areas of life. I want to pause briefly and highlight the word "all." Why might this short and simple word be so important in our consideration of the Great Commandment? The reason it is so important is due to a basic but significant reality of life. Absolutely everything we do, whether in thought or deed, begins within our heart, our soul, and our mind. What Christ is pointing out is that we are to love the Lord our God by all possible means. He not only desires but also deserves to reign supreme as King over every thought and deed of our lives, and yes, that also includes how we care for creation. If we truly love the Creator with our whole heart, soul, and mind, we will gladly take care of His creation.

The same applies to the second half of the commandment. Christ instructs that we should love other people just like He loved us. When we gladly care for creation we fulfill the calling to love our neighbor. So here, at the very core of the Christian faith, we find our divinely appointed obligation to express our love vertically to God and horizontally to our fellow man. If we carelessly participate in the degradation of God's handiwork then we must recognize that we are not demonstrating our love for Him to the fullness that He deserves. In the same way, when we show a lack of concern for what is happening to creation, this points to our lack of concern for people, since a hurting creation inevitably means hurting people. As Patricia Fagg has said so well:

47

*"If I fail to acknowledge that God has made the natural world and so treat His work with contempt, if I treat creation as if it were my own to do with as I please, if I deface creation and mar its ability to delight God and to bring Him glory, if I impair creation and its creatures so they cease to flourish in healthful balance, if I degrade my surroundings by greedily taking from creation and thoughtlessly tossing out the waste, then I put myself in the place of God and usurp His place as King. I am in rebellion against God. I have broken the two great commandments. I am not loving God. I am not loving my neighbor."[24]*

There is an additional thought we must also consider as we ponder the implications of the Great Commandment. In the world today there is a desperate need to elevate the degree to which we value and cherish human life, and as Christians we legitimately fight to uphold this value. When we recognize the unmistakable link between the well-being of people and the well-being of creation, our respect for the sanctity of human life provides even greater grounds for action. It gives us greater cause for moving forward, adding strength and clarity to our moral and ethical responsibilities, out of which a deeper respect for creation can be cultivated. What we see here is a win-win situation. When we elevate the degree to which we value our fellow man, we are also obliged to elevate the degree to which we value God's creation. The two go hand in hand.

As we conclude our consideration of the calling we have to love both God and our neighbor, I want to share one final thought. Dr. John Piper of Bethlehem Baptist Church once offered a fresh and powerful definition for the term "love", one which I will never forget.

*"Love is the overflow of my joy in God which gladly meets the needs of others."*[25]

From an environmental point of view, we live in a world where vast numbers of people face significant and increasing challenges in meeting their basic needs of food, water, and shelter. Caring for creation, in our quest to fulfill the Great Commandment, can be a very strategic means through which our love for Christ can be used to *"gladly meet the needs of others."*

Principle 3

# We care for creation because it can improve our efforts to fulfill the Great Commission

If Christ has called us to "gladly meet the needs of others" and if caring for creation can be a means of fulfilling the Great Commandment, our next step is to consider how this stream of thought can be applied to our understanding of the Great Commission. After all, these two mandates from our Savior stand before us as essential pillars to our Christian faith. What I hope we can discover is that much like a wedding, there is beauty and wholeness to be found when these two pillars are brought together.

The unfortunate fact is that the Church across the globe has done very little teaching on the topic of creation care. In many ways we could easily describe the Church as a sleeping giant on this issue. And yet, it is the one giant that has the most potential to make a meaningful difference. Fortunately there are some promising signs that this giant is waking up. Amongst Christians here in Kenya I am encouraged to see that an awakening is taking place, but to this day abundant evidence exists that the majority of our fellow believers are still sleeping on this issue. While thousands of agriculturally based communities enthusiastically attend Sunday services each week, most people in these communities will freely confess they have little or no understanding of what their faith in Christ means for their lives as farmers. What they learn at church on Sunday mornings often has no bearing on what people do in their fields during the rest of the week. As a result, most of these Christian farmers conduct their agricultural lives no differently than their non-Christian counterparts. The careless and often destructive practices carried out by non-believers are the very same practices exercised by Christians.

In the context of Africa we need to understand the significance of what is missing from this picture. Both foreign missionaries and local church leaders have worked for decades to introduce the gospel to a landscape filled with farmers and pastoralists, and unfortunately, that gospel has often said very little about what it means for the most common vocation on the continent. Yet this relationship with the land lies at the very core of how people live. It defines the cultures and customs of people groups almost everywhere we go. In the case of agriculture, the work devoted to farm-related activities sets the stage for how millions spend 80 percent of their time each week. If the gospel has not been shown to be relevant for what is the most common way of life on the African continent, then something significant has been left out of that gospel.

Let us consider how we might be able to transform this kind of situation by going back to remind ourselves of what is stated in the Great Commission. Here are the words of our Lord found in Matthew 28:19-20.

*"Therefore go and make disciples of all nations, baptizing them in the name of the Father and of the Son and of the Holy Spirit, and teaching them to obey everything I have commanded you."*

It is important to note that Jesus did not command that we go out and make mere converts. He called us to make disciples whose lives would revolutionize the world. Discipleship is what transforms people, communities, and whole countries, and discipleship lies at the heart of the Great Commission. If we are working with farmers, pastoralists, or fishermen, in the context of missions, and we are not addressing how the gospel of Christ should impact what is central to the lives and culture of those people, then we must acknowledge that our efforts are incomplete. We must recognize that we are not spreading the fullness of that gospel. Creation care can be an important part of teaching people to *"obey everything I have commanded you"* and to *"love your neighbor as yourself"*, accomplished by proper care and stewardship of the land.

As church leaders and missionaries who are dedicated to making disciples of all nations we need to inject some fresh ideas into our thinking. As we design our strategies, as we train and build up those who will lead the local indigenous church, and as we work with those who are new believers in Christ, here are some questions we might want to consider.

- For a farmer, pastoralist, or a fisherman who has received Christ as Savior, how should the fullness of gospel transformation be reflected in their day to day life and work?

- To see this kind of transformation take place, how would this change our strategies in ministering to the farmers, pastoralists, and fishermen of Africa?

- In a community where a degraded landscape is undermining the well-being of its people, how should a local pastor be trained to effectively address such issues? Do area Bible schools and seminaries offer any courses that equip pastors to fulfill this kind of role?

- For the missionary called to bring Christ to an unreached people who struggle with chronic hunger and poverty, what type of education would best prepare them for this kind of situation? What priorities should be emphasized by the mission agency to best reflect a holistic presentation of the gospel?

As we contend with these questions, we would also want to consider how to evaluate the degree to which we have succeeded in spreading this kind of holistic gospel. Do we measure our success only in the number of people attending Sunday services or in how many churches have been planted? Or should consideration be given to other factors as well?

These questions present us with a healthy but important challenge. As part of our efforts in discipleship we should do everything possible to train and build up Christian leaders and responsible communities who have a biblical worldview of creation, who see creation through God's eyes, and who recognize creation as a wonderful gift that needs to be nurtured for their own well-being and for the sake of their testimony. Working towards this goal is very consistent with

God's call for us to share the good news of Christ and to make disciples of all nations.

## Farming God's Way as a Model

Do we have ministry models that combine a strong discipleship orientation with a special focus on healing the creation? The exciting answer is yes, and we can point to a growing number of such ministries emerging around the world. Farming God's Way is one example that offers a very promising model. Based on a vision for producing Godly farmers, this movement has begun to sweep across Africa. Some encouraging aspects of this movement include the following:

- The first priority of Farming God's Way is to see that discipleship and biblical transformation is taking place in the hearts and minds of people. This foundation is the channel by which farmers receive a convicting motivation to change their behavior, encouraging them to honor the Creator by implementing a vision for restoring their soils and farms.

- Farming God's Way has enormous potential because it targets small scale farmers and the millions of people who are involved in the most common vocation on the continent.

- Planting this kind of vision for God-centered agricultural stewardship can be a strategic springboard for spiritual awakening and transformation into other realms of life. Once healing begins to take place in the agricultural domain, people can be encouraged to take the next steps. Are there other ways God wants to transform their community? Are there other creation care topics that need to be addressed?

• Farming God's Way, when properly implemented, has a proven track record to both heal degraded land and improve crop productivity at the same time. Many farmers have seen two, three, or even five-fold increases in their crop yields.

As Great Commission Christians consider the scarcity of resources, the hunger, poverty, and difficult challenges facing countless agricultural communities across Africa, our discipleship goals should be based on a vision for developing and multiplying godly farmers. Since Christ has encouraged us to be perfect, as our heavenly father is perfect (Matt 5:48), we should strive towards perfection in our efforts to help the people of Africa become excellent stewards of their land.

**For contact information and a detailed summary of Farming God's Way see Appendix 3**

### Creation-care as a New Frontier for Evangelical Missions

There is tremendous potential that emerges when we combine our obedience to the Great Commission and the Great Commandment with our obedience to care for creation. As the model of Farming God's Way demonstrates, this type of integrated approach stands before us as a new and exciting frontier for Christ-like witness in the 21st century. A remarkable opportunity exists to engage with the world in a way that is fresh and strategic. As we consider what this new frontier has to offer for the future we should also take a moment to reflect on the past. Are there missionaries who have gone before us who expressed concern about this topic and who pointed in this direction?

Paul Brand, a well-respected medical missionary is one such example. Growing up in South India, Paul tells a vivid story of how he developed strong convictions related to environmental stewardship. As a boy he recalls the meticulous care by which terraced rice paddies were maintained on the mountains in this region. Soil erosion was never a problem because forests were maintained, excellent standards were enforced on the paddies themselves, and rivers in the valleys ran clear. Thirty years later, however, after completing his training as a doctor, Paul returned to India as a missionary. When he visited the landscapes he had known as a child he was dismayed. The forests and terraces were gone; the rivers were choked with mud; and in some places only bare rock remained where healthy soil had once produced food. The senseless destruction that he witnessed led him to become a powerful advocate for tree planting and soil conservation during the rest of his missionary career. In his persuasive short story entitled "A Handful of Mud", Paul makes a compelling statement as follows:

> *"I would gladly give up medicine and surgery tomorrow if by so doing I could have some influence on policy with regard to mud and soil. The world will die from lack of soil and pure water long before it will die from lack of antibiotics or surgical skill and knowledge."* [26]

As a more contemporary missionary, Dr. Dan Fountain came to the same conclusion. Working in the Congo for 35 years as a physician, where he pioneered a very successful community based health care program, Dr. Fountain witnessed deforestation and other abuses on the land. Over the course of his ministry he became increasingly aware of a simple fact: healthy land was absolutely essential to the health of the people he was working with. This realization expanded his vision for health care, leading him to write a unique book entitled "Let's Restore Our Land".[27]

In this book we read about a local pastor named Simon, who takes it upon himself to lead his community in a number of land restoration efforts. By working to restore his own land first, Pastor Simon then uses simple teaching from Scripture to encourage others to do the same, helping them to also explore other land restoration issues within the broader community. In effect Pastor Simon becomes the development worker and the agent of transformation in his community. Like a missionary with boots on, he effectively brings a two handed gospel to his people. Their lives are enriched spiritually, and their effort to follow God's ways as obedient stewards brings physical renewal to their land. Imagine the transformation that would take place if church leaders all across Africa followed the example of Pastor Simon.

These two stories from veteran long-term missionaries point us toward an exciting direction as we seek to advance the gospel, and the opportunities for fruitful ministy abound. Here are a few examples of how this new frontier for missions could change the world.

- Millions of Christians across the globe have little or no understanding of the biblical roots for creation-care. Tremendous potential exists for discipling those believers, opening their eyes to a fresh and new understanding of their faith, and helping them to see how they can honor Christ in some very practical ways.

- As we consider the physical plight of the poor, including children and families who suffer from chronic food insecurity, this frontier offers tremendous potential to heal worn out landscapes, to stem the tide of poverty, to bless the malnourished, and to save the lives of those who might otherwise die of hunger.

- Mission agencies of all shapes and sizes are working to advance the cause of Christ around the world. Tremendous potential exists for these agencies to get on board by integrating creation care into the good work they already do.

- Many missionaries have a special calling to bring the gospel to unreached people groups. These people often live in very remote areas, where environmental conditions are harsh, or where landscapes are heavily degraded. Tremendous potential exists to spread the gospel among these people through creative outreach efforts like Farming God's Way.

- Many of us have unbelieving friends who are part of the secular environmental movement. Tremendous potential exists to strengthen our witness to such people, who have often rejected the Church because we have been so quiet on this topic. We can bless these individuals with a very legitimate foundation which supports the passions they already possess, but which also guides them to Christ and allows them to express those passions in a way that brings glory to God.

- In Christian colleges and universities around the world it is encouraging to see more and more students expressing interest in environmental topics. This new frontier for missions offers tremendous potential to mobilize and enlist young Christians everywhere whose hearts are incubating and developing a growing concern about creation care.

In the context of missions it is clear that we need to add a new type of missionary to the team. For decades we have seen wonderful work accomplished by the hands of medical missionaries and by those who plant churches, train pastors or who translate the scriptures. It is time that we combine these collective efforts into a cohesive and holistic approach that does not separate the spiritual from the physical. The world desperately needs Great Commission missionaries with expertise in forestry, fisheries, and sustainable agriculture. It needs godly men and women who are trained in appropriate technology, wildlife conservation, water resource management, environmental education, and other similar fields. Armed with the gospel of Christ these professionals could advance God's kingdom and have an impact that we can only begin to imagine.

Given the possibilities outlined above, this new frontier requires that we think carefully about embracing and defining a new category of missionary. I am very thankful for the thoughtful work of Lowell Bliss and his book entitled *"Environmental Missions: Planting Churches and Trees"*. As someone who served as a church planting missionary for 14 years in India and Pakistan, it is remarkable to read his testimony of how he developed the same convictions as Dr. Brand and Dr. Fountain. Bliss has provided us with a thoughtful definition for this new category of missionary.

> *"Environmental missionaries are those sent cross culturally to labor with Christ – the Creator, Sustainer, and Redeemer of all creation – in caring for the environment and making disciples among all peoples."* [28]

We should care for creation because we want to be faithful to the Great Commission, because we want to disciple and bring healing to both people and their land, and because we want to bless people both spiritually and physically. Hope for eternity combined with hope for today should be reflected in all our Great Commission endeavors.

Principle 4

# We care for creation because our dominion over the earth was meant to honor Christ

As we appreciate the truth that creation care blends together with our mandate to live out the Great Commandment and the Great Commission, we can build further credibility onto this idea by looking carefully into the concept of dominion. What did God really intend when He allowed mankind to exercise dominion over the earth?

John Calvin offers some excellent thoughts on this reality, pointing out that God's intentions from the beginning were very clear. Mankind was to exercise his dominion as a good steward of creation. What we see in Calvin's quote below is an expectation that certain standards of care are adhered to, standards which do not lead to the injury of the land, but rather, standards which maintain and even improve the land.

> "The custody of the garden was given in charge to Adam, to show that we possess the things which God has committed to our hands, on the condition, that being content with the frugal and moderate use of

*them, we should take care of what shall remain. Let him who possesses a field, so partake of its yearly fruits, that he may not suffer the ground to be injured by negligence; but let him endeavor to hand it down to posterity as he received it, or even better cultivated. Let him so feed on its fruits, that he neither dissipates it by luxury, nor permits it to be marred or ruined by neglect....Let everyone regard himself as the steward of God in all things which he possesses."*[29]

If we are to reach a proper conclusion, as John Calvin has, about the nature of our dominion over creation, we must look carefully at two key passages in Genesis, and these passages should be examined together. They reveal not only the truth of mankind's God-given authority at the dawn of time, but they underscore that along with that authority came significant responsibility.

*"Then God said, 'Let us make man in our image, in our likeness, and let them rule over the fish of the sea and the birds of the air, over the livestock, over all the earth, and over all the creatures that move along the ground.'"* (Genesis 1:26)

*"The Lord God took the man and put him in the Garden of Eden to work it and take care of it."* (Genesis 2:15)

It is unfortunate that Genesis 1:26 has often been interpreted in isolation to Genesis 2:15, leading to a predominant view held by many Christians around the world. This view is based on a simple but dangerous assumption, the mistaken idea that God created the world solely for man's benefit. The commonly held belief that corresponds with this assumption is that humans may use the earth as we see fit. Many believers adhere to this assumption subconsciously, while numerous others use the Genesis 1:26 passage more directly, to justify their lifestyles and their belief that God has allowed mankind to have unchallenged dominion over creation. Nothing could be more misguided or wrong.

Secular thinking has also played a significant role in distorting our perspective of dominion. The result has been a worldview accompanied by behaviors and decisions that can be more accurately described as domination as opposed to a true biblical understanding of dominion. This worldly perspective often looks to the creation as nothing more than a giant supermarket that supplies the raw materials for man's endeavors. You pull up to the loading dock, fill your truck with whatever resources creation has to offer, and drive off without any consideration to what damage may have resulted to landscapes or people when those resources were harvested. And we simply assume that another load of resources will be readily available when we return.

Fortunately we know from Scripture that creation is far more than a supermarket filled with raw materials and supplies. In the true biblical sense, our relationship with creation was intended to be much like that of a God-fearing king who exercises loving care across his kingdom, a king who is a servant to his people and who rules with righteousness and justice. This is clearly seen in God's expectations of earthly kings in the Old Testament. Man's dominion from a biblical point of view should be conducted in a manner that pleases God, that brings glory to His name, and that benefits the whole of creation. Yes, we do have dominion, but we should not exercise that dominion as we see fit. We should exercise it as God sees fit.

This line of reasoning is confirmed and becomes clear when Genesis 2 is examined. The very first thing God did was to create the heavens and the earth, and remarkably, the very first task assigned to Adam was to "work" and "take care of" the Garden (vs. 15). This was mankind's very first job description. Other English translations of this verse use the following phrases: "to dress it and to keep it", "to tend and care for it", "to serve and preserve it". The ability to exercise dominion over creation should be viewed, therefore, as a divinely appointed privilege and responsibility. We were created for Christ-like dominion, not greedy, exploitative, or selfish domination.

Now that we have established that our dominion should be Christ-like, it raises an important question. What characterizes worldly dominion, and how would that be different from a Christ-like approach? Here are several characteristics that I suggest could describe a worldly perspective in utilizing the resources of creation.

- It is often oriented towards greed and exploitation, with profit usually being the goal of exploitation.

- It puts current needs first, gives little consideration to long-term impacts, and is often willing to deplete or exhaust the resources of creation for short-term gain.

- It has a primary focus on money, the sale and/or purchase of as many goods as possible, and it seeks to earn as much as possible with as little work as possible.

- It is never content, always needs more, and promotes the secular values of unbridled consumerism and materialism.

- It shows little regard for the poor and frequently ignores the needs of current or future generations.

- It causes lasting damage to the creation.

We can easily agree that this kind of orientation brings no honor to Christ. It is a radical departure from our biblical values and it is downright idolatrous. One might ask, "Does God give us any clear indication in the Scriptures about how He might react to this type of selfish exploitation?" Yes He does, and a rather stark example can be found in Isaiah 37:23-24. Here we see God chastising King Sennacherib for his arrogant deeds that have led to the destruction of forests and water.

*"Who is it you have insulted and blasphemed? Against whom have you raised your voice and lifted your eyes in pride? Against the Holy One of Israel! By your messengers you have heaped insults on the Lord. And you have said, 'With my many chariots I have ascended the heights of the mountains, the utmost heights of Lebanon. I have cut down its tallest cedars, the choicest of its pines. I have reached its remotest heights, the finest of its forests. I have dug wells in foreign lands and drunk the water there. With the soles of my feet I have dried up all the streams of Egypt.' "*

The conclusion that we draw from this passage could not be more obvious. When we use creation in a manner that leads to its injury or ruination, it is a sinful and blasphemous insult to God, especially when the attitude accompanying such abuse is flavored with pride. While this comes as no surprise based on what we have already learned, we should make note that there is severity and significance to what King Sennacherib has done. God does not view this as a single insult. He views it as insults heaped upon insults.

In contrast to these reflections that identify a sinful approach to man's dominion, what would a God-centered expression of our dominion look like? Let us now turn the tables and identify some characteristics that reflect the spirit of Christ. I would propose the following:

First, I would offer that Christ-like dominion would categorically reject the temptations of greed and materialism. This would follow in close keeping with Christ's words of warning found in Luke 12:15: *"Watch out! Be on your guard against all kinds of greed; a man's life does not consist in the abundance of his possessions."*

Second, Christ-like dominion would demonstrate a respect for God as the Owner of all things found within the vineyard of creation. The parable of the Tenants in Matthew 21:33-41 is very instructive here. We are reminded in this story of how the wicked tenants, hired to manage the vineyard, displayed great disrespect to the landowner. Many of the master's servants were beaten or killed by the tenants, and eventually they turned upon and killed the master's own son. Such treatment of what belonged to God was an abomination.

Third, it would rule over creation with a commitment to righteousness, justice, and mercy, in keeping with God's desires as seen in passages like Micah 6:8. *"He has shown you O man, what is good. And what does the Lord require of you? To act justly, and to love mercy, and to walk humbly with your God."* Not only does Christ-like dominion pursue what is true, fair, and kind, but it is exemplified by humility and is oriented towards what God desires, unlike the insulting example of King Sennacherib.

Fourth, and in keeping with the passage from Micah, a dominion that glorifies God would give priority to the poor and needy. Working to improve and heal creation for the sake of the poor would be on the top of our agendas, as opposed to placing such concerns at the bottom of the list. Christ reminds us of our obligation to the disadvantaged in the parable of the sheep and goats, which calls us to feed the hungry, give drink to the thirsty, and clothe the naked (Matthew 25:31-46). In fact, the authenticity of our faith is revealed by our response to such needs.

Fifth, when we look to the parable of the talents in Matthew 25:14-23, we can conclude that Christ-like dominion would strive to enhance creation's bounty. It would fight against trends where creation's abundance is fading or in decline. In this story the master praises the servants who use their resources wisely by multiplying what had been given to them, and he condemns the one who gained nothing by hiding his talent in the ground. All the resources of creation should be viewed as "talents" which have been entrusted to our care. Our goal should be to use them wisely, so that Christ will have ample reason to express his approval by saying *"Well done, good and faithful servant."* (vs. 23)

Finally, we can also understand how all these characteristics fall under the overarching umbrella of Christ's command to love God wholeheartedly and to love our neighbors as ourselves, as we have seen in principle two. Christ-like dominion keeps the interests of both current and future generations in mind. It is a dominion of nurture and care. It pursues the quality and character of both people and their land, properly stewarding the animals, farms, trees and water. It is not careless, it does not waste, and it is able to celebrate and enjoy the fruits of creation without destroying its fruitfulness. This was God's design for mankind from the beginning.

Principle 5

# We care for creation because it suffers from our sin

In spite of our calling to exercise Christ-like dominion over creation, we all recognize that we have fallen woefully short of the mark. When Adam and Eve turned their back on God in the Garden of Eden their rebellion opened a door to the most highly contagious infection we have ever known. The tentacles of sin polluted all of mankind and the entire world under his domain. Not only were Adam and Eve denied fruit from the Tree of Life, they were banished from the garden altogether, and life became difficult and painful (Genesis 3:22-24). When God expelled Adam and Eve from the garden He was sending a clear message that the consequences of sin are enormous and all-pervasive. The whole of creation has suffered as a result.

In the midst of this suffering we regularly observe concerned leaders, institutions, scientists and others around the globe voicing urgent messages about environmental decay. While it is useful to acknowledge the severity of the problem, unfortunately something significant is usually missing from those voices. What these reports fail to highlight is the root cause of such decay. Christians who share a concern for what is happening need to present a very honest and straightforward question to the world: "What is the primary and underlying cause of our environmental problems?" After all, the quest to solve any problem should begin with identifying the root cause.

Imagine if we posed this question to the Environmental Protection Agency (EPA) in the United States or the top leaders of the United Nation's Environmental Program (UNEP), whose world headquarters are located here in Nairobi. What kind of answers might we expect? I can guarantee that we will not get a clear answer as to the root cause, but we will get a host of other answers.

Some will say it is mostly a problem of poverty, ignorance, and a lack of education. Others will point the finger at overpopulation, poor governance, or the lack of political will and proper regulatory policies. Still others would say that air pollution, overfishing, deforestation and destructive farming practices are very widespread. They would highlight the lack of economic incentives, the lack of funding to properly address such issues, and the list would go on. Now granted, we can agree that there is partial truth in most of these reasons. But when you boil it all down, and when the rubber meets the road, what is the ultimate cause? As Christians we all know the answer, but at this point it would be prudent to turn and read it straight from Scripture. In the following passages it is interesting to note the strong overtones of a groaning creation.

*"Hear the word of the Lord, you Israelites, because the Lord has a charge to bring against you who live in the land: 'There is no faithfulness, no love, no acknowledgement of God in the land. There is only cursing, lying and murder, stealing and adultery; they break all bounds, and bloodshed follows bloodshed. Because of this the land mourns, and all who live in it waste away; the beasts of the field and the birds of the air and the fish of the sea are dying.' " (Hosea 4:1-3)*

*"What man is wise enough to understand this? Who has been instructed by the Lord and can explain it? Why has the land been ruined and laid waste like a desert that no one can cross? The Lord said, 'It is because they have forsaken my law, which I set before them; they have not obeyed or followed my law.' " (Jeremiah 9:12-13)*

*"How long will the land lie parched and the grass in every field be withered? Because those who live in it are wicked, the animals and birds have perished." (Jeremiah 12:4)*

Indeed we live in a world filled with pain, broken relationships, cancer, corruption, racism, human trafficking, refugees fleeing their home countries, and of course, environmental destruction. As painful as all this suffering is, we can take solace in the fact that the Bible's diagnosis for this litany of problems is right on target: *"There is no faithfulness, no love, no acknowledgement of God in the land" (Hosea 4:1).* Fundamentally, the root cause of all this brokenness is man's rebellion against God. Environmental problems are rooted in the spiritual problem of sin. This is where Christians need to boldly step forward and proclaim the truth.

As one who suffered life threatening cancer there is an enduring principle that I quickly learned to appreciate. We all recognize that a proper cure for a disease cannot be administered without a proper diagnosis. What is beautiful about Scripture is that it not only gives an accurate diagnosis for the root cause, it also provides the most promising prescription for a cure. And that cure is found in the person of Christ, who came to earth for the expressed purpose of defeating the destructive and polluting power of sin. Titus 2:11-14 provides an exhilarating summary of this reality, which outlines the essence of the gospel.

> "For the grace of God that brings salvation has appeared to all men. It teaches us to say "No" to ungodliness and worldly passions, and to live self-controlled, upright, and godly lives, while we wait for the blessed hope – the glorious appearing of our great God and Savior, Jesus Christ, who gave himself for us to redeem us from all wickedness and to purify for himself a people that are his very own, eager to do what is good."

Christians are called to consider an appropriate response to the environmental problems of our day and this passage is filled with wonderful implications. We are encouraged to vigorously reject the secular passions of this world. We are called to resist the river of materialism that sweeps us towards greed and a loss of self-control, which so often brings harm, ruin and tragic consequences to both people and creation. And as we struggle against this tide we are strengthened in our resolve by the hope we have in the return of our Lord. He is coming to reconcile all things to Himself. This gives us courage to stand firm, and as we stand we must strive for righteousness and eagerly do that which is good. Caring for creation is just one of the many good things we should be doing with enthusiasm.

So in the final analysis we must recognize that there is one primary and most promising solution to alleviating the crisis that we see in creation. Since our environmental problems are rooted in sin, and since Christ came to earth for the expressed purpose of dealing with sin, He is the first resource we must turn to. The sea-change of attitude and behavior that is so desperately needed cannot come from an approach to the environment that ignores the Creator, that leaves out the very One who can convict and transform the hearts of people. He is the One who can give us victory over the sin in our lives. Our most promising solution in this crisis is found in the life-changing and sin conquering power of an active and maturing relationship with Jesus Christ.

With this truth in mind we can now see how the Church has an unmistakable and critical role to play. More than any other group on the planet, God has equipped the Church with not only the best tools but also the best reasons to stand up and make a difference. While the fullness of the cure that is needed will not take place until Christ's return, we should take full advantage of the sin-conquering power that He offers in the here and now. We should humbly invite Him to clean up the pollution in our lives and in our world. Every effort we make to this end will honor and glorify Him.

James Gustave (Gus) Speth, a well-known leader and environmental lawyer in the US, once made a brilliant statement that confessed the limitations of mankind, and of science, in solving these issues. His remarks highlight the very reason why the Church needs to get involved.

> "I used to think that top environmental problems were biodiversity loss, ecosystem collapse and climate change. I thought that thirty years of good science could address these problems. I was wrong. The top environmental problems are selfishness, greed and apathy, and to deal with these we need a cultural and spiritual transformation. And we scientists don't know how to do that." [30]

Principle 6

# We care for creation because God calls us to glorify Him in all things

There are some words we use so commonly in Christianity that at times the significance of those terms fade from our memory. We repeat them so frequently that we often fail to reflect carefully on their meaning. One such term is "glory" or "glorify." We verbalize this term in our prayers, in our worship songs, and we often hear it in sermons given from the pulpit. So when we talk about the concept of glorifying God, what does it really mean to glorify Him in all things?

Christians understand this concept as a divine calling to live our lives in a way that honors God. More precisely, we pursue the goal of conducting ourselves in a manner that demonstrates, displays, and reflects the immeasurable goodness of God. Enjoying the excellence of our Creator and also demonstrating His excellence to others is central to our faith. It defines the very reason for which we were created, and this ultimate purpose for life was not meant to be expressed halfheartedly, only in piecemeal or limited fashion. It was meant to be expressed fully throughout all dimensions of our lives. We see this reality expressed very well in Paul's writings to the churches in Colosse and Corinth, where he encourages Christians to become mature and live their lives in a manner pleasing to the Lord.

*"And we pray this in order that you may live a life worthy of the Lord and may please him in every way: bearing fruit in every good work, growing in the knowledge of God..." (Colossians 1:10)*

*"So whether you eat or drink or whatever you do, do it all for the glory of God." (I Corinthians 10:31)*

We must make careful note here to the all surpassing and comprehensive nature of these commands. In "every way" and in "every good work" and even in the most common and ordinary activities of everyday life, such as eating and drinking, God calls us to be representatives of His excellence. In a world where hunger abounds, when we eat or drink with a complaining spirit, when we grumble that the tea was not hot enough, the orange juice was not cold enough, or that the food did not taste as good as we had hoped, we can humbly admit that we are not honoring the one who has provided for our sustenance.

So here is the important consideration that deserves our full attention: If God is interested in every aspect of our lives, and even the smallest details in how we eat or drink, and if He is concerned that we should use every opportunity to demonstrate His goodness and greatness to others, then surely He must be interested in how we care for His creation. Surely He is interested in how we manage our forests, how we make use of the fish in our lakes and oceans, how we strive to minimize pollution from our automobiles and factories, and how we use farmland to produce food. Surely He is interested in our efforts to live in healthy balance with wild animals, birds, and other creatures, so they too can bring Him glory and carry out the purpose for which they were created.

We should strive to honor God to the best of our ability in all areas of life and at all times. In today's world where so much damage has already been inflicted upon creation we need to walk circumspectly, and we must continually uphold some very important questions as we strive to live out the fullness of these commands from Scripture:

- How can I best glorify God as I use these resources from his creation or as I manage this land?

- What is the best course of action as I strive to please the Lord in "every way" and as I consider my responsibility to my neighbor, my community, and to future generations?

- What would Jesus want me to do as I face the wide variety of choices, situations, and even temptations in the often complex process of relating to His creation?

In each and every decision that we make, in each and every activity that we undertake, whether small or large, the world desperately cries out for people who will give serious consideration to such questions. The individual who picks up a small piece of garbage on the street to keep his town clean can demonstrate the spirit of Colossians 1:10 and I

Corinthians 10:31 to the same extent as the person who organizes his community to develop a plan for reforestation.

We should also note that since God is the one who provides us with so many good things from His creation, we have an obligation to always be grateful to Him. A grateful heart is a heart which brings glory to God, and I would point out that such a heart is also one that is more inclined to tread carefully upon creation. As professor Stanley Jaki once said:

*"Man abuses nature most rudely when he fails to find in it a pedestal to praise God and to be grateful to Him."*[31]

As we continue reflecting on these passages I find it very interesting that Paul uses the topic of food *("whether you eat or drink or whatever you do")* to make His point about glorifying God. Farming and food production happen to be some of the most significant ways in which human beings impact the creation. The methods by which we grow, harvest, or capture food have often been destructive and unsustainable, as demonstrated across farming landscapes in a place like Kenya. Forests have been stripped, and both soil and life-giving water have been washed away, significantly reducing the productive capability of the land, a scenario that has been repeated across many parts of the world.

This raises some important questions: How can we fully glorify God in our eating and drinking? Can we be more comprehensive in honoring Him and expressing our gratefulness for the landscapes that sustain us? Yes we can. As Christians we already do this to some degree. Whenever we sit down to enjoy a plate of food we regularly carry out a noble task. We pray and thank the Lord for His provision, and we often remember those who may not be able to find enough food for that day. This is to be commended. It is what God wants us to do.

However, we should also give careful thought to the bigger picture. We must realize that a plate of food represents the last step of the agricultural process, and agriculture is a long progression of many steps. Is God interested in each of those steps? Would he be concerned about the process itself? Multiple activities have taken place prior to serving that plate of food. Land has been tilled, seed has been planted, crops have been sprayed with chemicals, fish have been caught in a net, a cow has been slaughtered, the food transported over long distances, etc.

If we went to a restaurant and during the meal discovered that the meat we were eating came from a goat stolen from a poor man, we would be outraged. If we discovered that the wheat flour purchased from the supermarket was grown by a commercial farmer who had illegally obtained land by evicting a group of peasant farmers, we would be equally outraged. If a rare portion of native forest was cleared for growing a plantation of bananas, and the employees of that farm faced health risks because they had to apply pesticides without protective gloves or clothing, we would refuse to purchase bananas from that farm.

The lesson is clear. God has instructed us to please him in "in every way", to bear fruit in "every good work", and to glorify him in how we eat or drink. We should honor Him in the larger picture of food production and not merely at the end when the plate of food is served. We should pursue excellence in all steps and in all things, from beginning to end. This includes the entire process of planting, growing, harvesting and producing what we eat or drink. If people are mistreated or if the bounty of our Lord's creation is being marred or diminished in the processes by which we obtain our food, we fail to glorify him as we should.

Principle 7

# We care for creation because God Himself cares for creation

If God has called us to glorify him in how we care for creation, we can build further credibility onto that concept by recognizing that God himself cares for creation. When the Israelites were suffering in bondage at the hands of the Egyptians, a very famous story begins to unfold in the third chapter of Exodus, where God appears to Moses in a burning bush because He has determined to rescue His people. He is concerned about their suffering as slaves, and His desire is to rescue them from a place of misery and bring them to a place of beauty and abundance. This is a brand new home; a place within God's creation so bountiful that the description provided in the Scripture burns a memory within our minds that we can never forget. The *"good and spacious land"* which God has selected as a blessing for His people is "a land flowing with milk and honey..." (Exodus 3:8). The glorious imagery of the Garden of Eden now reappears, and the abundant life that Adam and Eve were meant to enjoy is being offered to the entire nation of Israel. As we will note later in this book, a beautiful picture like this emerges yet a third time, at the very end of Scripture.

What is interesting in this account about the Promised Land is that God holds a particular affection and interest for this place. After spending 40 years wandering in the desert as a result of their rebellious ways, here in Deuteronomy the Israelites are about to cross the Jordan river to enter the land of Canaan.

> *"Love the Lord your God and keep his requirements, his decrees, his laws and his commands always. Remember today that your children were not the ones who saw and experienced the discipline of the Lord your God...the signs he performed and the things he did in the heart of Egypt..." (Deuteronomy 11:1-3)*

> *"Observe therefore all the commands I am giving you today, so that you may have the strength to go in and take over the land that you are crossing the Jordan to possess, and so that you may live long in the land that the Lord swore to your forefathers to give them...a land flowing with milk and honey. The land you are entering to take over is not like the land of Egypt, from which you have come, where you planted your seed and irrigated it by foot as in a vegetable garden. But the land you are crossing the Jordan to take possession of is a land of mountains and valleys that drinks rain from heaven. It is a land the Lord your God cares for; the eyes of the Lord your God are continually on it from the beginning of the year to its end." (Deuteronomy 11:8-12)*

There are several important lessons to learn here. First of all, the ability to *"live long in the land"*, the ability to enjoy the fullness of its blessings, comes with a serious condition. The people must be obedient to the Great Commandment. They must love the Lord with all of their hearts, and they must do so all of the time, on a continual basis. In the verses that follow God warns them, highlighting the harsh consequences of disobedience, and how the abundance of the land will be removed if the people fail to obey.

The second important observation is the unique way in which God watches over this land. Not only is the Promised Land an exceedingly beautiful place, drinking rain from heaven, but it is also a place that God cares for, and He cares for it all of the time, on a continual basis. If God cares for the land *"from the beginning of the year to its end"* then what are the implications for God's people? If God has made us in His image and if He cares for his own creation, then by all means God's people should be following in his footsteps.

Having seen this example of God's perpetual watchfulness over the land there are other passages in Scripture that highlight this truth. Psalm 65:9-13 provides a nice parallel to what is said in Deuteronomy. God is not only someone who cares for the land but He actually works to enrich what is provided from that land.

> "You care for the land and water it; you enrich it abundantly. The streams of God are filled with water to provide the people with grain, for so you have ordained it. You drench its furrows and level its ridges; you soften it with showers and bless its crops. You crown the year with your bounty, and your carts overflow with abundance. The grasslands of the dessert overflow; the hills are clothed with gladness. The meadows are covered with flocks and the valleys are mantled with grain; they shout for joy and sing."

Note again the vivid language used here, and the combination of mankind with a landscape welling up with water, plenty of grain, and luxuriant pasture for livestock, all a result of God's providential care.

This theme is emphasized once more in another striking passage found later on in the Old Testament. In Job 12:7-9 all the layers are stripped away and we get to the very core of what God does on behalf of His creation. Every breath of every creature and every expression of life on the planet is upheld and sustained by His hand.

> "But ask the animals, and they will teach you, or the birds of the air, and they will tell you; or speak to the earth, and it will teach you, or let the fish of the sea inform you. Which of all these does not know that the hand of the Lord has done this? In his hand is the life of every creature and the breath of all mankind."

This mention of creation's complete dependence upon God is a reality about the universe that is not taught in the Old Testament alone. It spans the whole Bible.

When we finally move on to the New Testament we then read the most succinct and powerful declaration that binds together everything that all these passages have been saying.

> "In the past God spoke to our forefathers through the prophets at many times and in various ways, but in these last days he has spoken to us by his Son, whom he appointed heir of all things, and through whom he made the universe. The Son is the radiance of

*God's glory and the exact representation of his being,*
*sustaining all things by his powerful word."*
*(Hebrews 1:1-3)*

Here we see Christ as the main channel through which God has spoken to men. He is affirmed once again as being the Creator of all things, including the whole universe. On top of this He holds all these things together. Our life and breath at this moment is made possible because of His loving care, and without His unceasing and sustaining power the whole of creation as we know it would fall apart. This truth reveals an important lesson for the purposes of this book.

If God continually works to care for and sustain His own creation, and if we are the continual beneficiaries of His work, through the milk that we drink, the honey that we taste, and the grain we use to bake our bread, then we have a twofold obligation. The first is to uphold our sincere appreciation for His provision, and the second is tied very closely with it. We must make sure that we do not undermine the various processes He has put in place to make that provision possible. How great our offense must be when we behave in a manner that disrupts or damages the sustaining flow of work that God performs through His creation, and how great His joy must be when we gladly commit ourselves to care for His creation on a continual basis, just like He does.

Principle 8

# We care for creation because it was God's will for all things to exist and have their being

When a dignitary such as the president of a powerful nation or the Secretary General of the United Nations stands before the press, their words and desires are quickly heard around the world. What is stated holds weight and significance because such leaders can alter the circumstances that affect the lives of people. When it comes to creation, Christians have often overlooked the significance of the words stated at the very beginning of time and by a far more important dignitary. Creation exists, as we know it, because God spoke it into existence. Let us remind ourselves what was actually stated by God as found in Genesis 1.

> *"And God said, 'Let there be light,' and there was light. God saw that the light was good, and he separated the light from the darkness." (vs. 3-4)*

> *"And God said, 'Let there be an expanse between the waters, to separate water from water....God called the expanse 'sky.' " (vs. 6-8)*

*"And God said, 'Let the water under the sky be gathered to one place, and let dry ground appear.' And it was so. God called the dry ground 'land,' and the gathered waters he called 'seas' "* (vs. 9-10)

*"Then God said, 'Let the land produce vegetation: seed bearing plants and trees on the land that bear fruit with seed in it, according to their various kinds.' And it was so."* (vs. 11)

*"And God said, 'Let there be lights in the expanse of the sky to separate the day from the night, and let them serve as signs to mark seasons and days and years...'"* (vs. 14)

*"And God said, 'Let the water teem with living creatures, and let birds fly above the earth across the expanse of the sky.' So God created the great creatures of the sea and every living and moving thing with which the water teems, according to their kinds, and every winged bird according to its kind."* (vs. 20-21)

*"And God said, 'Let the land produce living creatures according to their kinds: livestock, creatures that move along the ground, and wild animals, each according to its kind.' And it was so."* (vs. 24)

*"Then God said, 'Let us make man in our image, in our likeness, and let them rule over the fish of the sea and the birds of the air, over the livestock, over all the earth, and over all the creatures that move along the ground.' "* (vs. 26)

I have taken the time to list these verses for a reason. As familiar as these passages might be, we must give them thoughtful consideration. We must remind ourselves that this serves as God's State of the Union address. This was His opening message to mankind. God spoke light into existence, the stars in the universe, the water and dry land, a dazzling variety of plants, trees and vegetation to carpet the landscapes of the world, followed by an equally amazing collection of fish, birds, animals, and finally, mankind. As Moses was inspired to write the Torah, God wanted to communicate to people about what happened first and how it came to pass. This glorious world came about as a result of His spoken declarations.

Such declarations made by God should not be viewed as insignificant or given less attention than they deserve. Neither should they be compared to human pronouncements made by a mere president or earthly king. They stand in a class entirely on their own by the virtue of the One who is making them, and for that reason they carry incalculable authority and importance, far beyond what is common to man. The One who made the universe is speaking, and He is announcing His personal intentions for what creation will be like. Everything He made is a legitimate expression of His spoken desire. All things exist because He wants them to exist. We see this affirmed very clearly by Revelation 4:11.

> "You are worthy, our Lord and God, to receive glory and honor and power, for you created all things, and by your will they were created and have their being."

Since this is the means through which creation came into being (via the spoken will of God), the people of God have an undeniable obligation to fully embrace what God wills and desires. To revere and to respect what He has created is an obvious and appropriate response, and all parts of creation must be recognized as having inherent value on their own, because God values them. I may not have a conclusive answer to the question about how we should view things like malarial mosquitoes, tsetse flies and infectious bacteria in this fallen world filled with sin, but I do know that we should care for creation because God intended the richness and diversity of everything that He made to exist and have their being. If God values the rhino, the elephant, the cheetah, the tuna and the dolphins, the trees and flowers, the hawks and eagles and the birds of the forest, then we should value them. We should do our utmost to make sure that future generations can witness, enjoy and receive inspiration from all the wonders of God's creation.

Principle 9

# We care for creation because God delights in the work of His hands, and so do His people

I f it is God's will for all things to exist and have their being, this gives us good reason to wonder what kind of opinion God holds about the things He has made. One of the pleasures of being an artist or craftsman is to step back after many hours of work, and to enjoy a sense of fulfillment in a job well done. The degree of satisfaction experienced is directly proportional to the degree of excellence seen in the final product. In the case of creation, after declaring the goodness of what He had made on six previous occasions, the Master Artist steps back to analyze the entire scene, and here is the assessment He gives in Genesis 1:31.

*"God saw all that he had made, and it was very good."*

Delight in a job well done is expressed, the final product is magnificent beyond human understanding, and so is the proportion of God's pleasure when He pronounces it to be "very good". God takes great joy in His creation, He holds a high opinion of that which He has made, and yes, He enjoys creation just like we do. The author of Psalm 104:31 reinforces this truth when he writes:

*"May the glory of the Lord endure forever; may the Lord rejoice in his works."*

The implications for creation care are clear. If this is the kind of response that God gives to His creation, it goes without saying that we should have a corresponding response, one that both marvels at and carefully maintains the excellent work of the most renowned Artist in the universe. At the same time we must also see the connection between the goodness of God's creation and the innumerable good benefits it holds for people. This is not just a famous painting hanging on a wall collecting dust in an art gallery. Creation is a three-dimensional reality filled with an abundance of living and non-living things, including soil, rocks, the sun and sky, all of which bring delight to God and which serve as the essential building blocks for sustaining life. When we put these realities together we can start to appreciate why God pronounced His creation to be "very good".

While Genesis 1:31 and Psalm 104:31 provide a good introduction to the idea that God delights in His creation, there are other key passages of Scripture that also deserve to be highlighted. In his book, *"The Pleasures of God"*, Dr. John Piper has done a brilliant job in outlining the reasons why God rejoices in what He has made. For those interested in a more thorough discourse, I highly recommend that you read Chapter 3 in his book. Let me borrow from his work and summarize some of those reasons in my own words.

To begin our exploration of this concept, one of the most important reasons God delights in His creation is that it serves as a continual testimony to His glory and splendor. We saw this earlier in Psalm 19:1 which states that the *"Heavens declare the glory of God; the skies proclaim the work of his hands."* The excellence of God is reflected in the excellence of His creation, and God is pleased to see creation speaking so clearly and consistently as it sends out this powerful message of truth to the whole world.

In keeping with this theme, a second reason God is able to delight in His creation is the fact that it also speaks clearly about His wisdom. Once again, we can turn to the book of Psalms to see this truth.

> *"How many are your works, O Lord! In wisdom you made them all; the earth is full of your creatures. There is the sea, vast and spacious, teeming with creatures beyond number - living things both large and small."* (Psalm 104:24-25)

In today's world of modern advancements it is all too easy to disregard a significant reality in life. Things like cells, light and matter, and the intricate details of their structure still defy the fields of science. As humans we continue to be baffled when we look into a microscope or a telescope. Our best scientists understand these things in part, but many of them would confess that they have only scratched the surface. The creation displays complexity and creativity beyond our understanding, with seemingly endless numbers of insects, birds, animals and plants, not to mention the uncountable billions of stars in a universe of seemingly endless space. All these point to the unmistakable wisdom of God.

Applying this truth in a practical way here in Kenya is something I often enjoy doing in the field of forestry. One question that is commonly raised by the local people is stated as follows: "Why should we plant indigenous trees?" My response is to direct these people to our Creator by saying: "It was God in His wisdom who blessed our nation with over 1,000 species of trees. If this is what God has done, then we too should be planting the same trees."

In the same way that creation speaks a consistent message about God's wisdom, Isaiah 40:26 shows that it also speaks clearly about His power.

> *"Lift your eyes and look to the heavens: Who created all these? He who brings out the starry host one by one, and calls them each by name. Because of his great power and mighty strength, not one of them is missing."*

There is unmistakable evidence shown to us every day that the power we see in nature, the power we see in the sun, the power we see in the waves and wind and in places like Victoria Falls – all these are powers that vastly exceed our power as humans. As Dr. Piper has stated so eloquently:

> *"What is this universe but the lavish demonstration of the incredible, incomparable, unimaginable exuberance and wisdom and power and greatness of God! What a God he must be!"[32]*

At this point we might be tempted to think that we have completed our exploration of why God delights in His creation, but there is more. Not only does creation speak, it also sings. The reality that creation acclaims and brings praise to its Creator is clearly seen in passages like Psalm 148:3-10 and 150:1-6. These are just two of many examples to be found in the Psalms.

> *"Praise him sun and moon, praise him all you shining stars. Praise him you highest heavens and you waters above the skies. Let them praise the name of the Lord, for he commanded and they were created...Praise the Lord from the earth, you great sea creatures and all ocean depths, lightening and hail, snow and clouds, stormy winds that do his bidding, you mountains and all hills, fruit trees and all cedars, wild animals and all cattle, small creatures and flying birds..."*

> *"Praise the Lord. Praise God in his sanctuary; praise him in his mighty heavens. Praise him for his acts of power; praise him for his surpassing greatness...Let everything that has breath praise the Lord."*

As we reflect on these passages we must keep in mind that when we praise something we do so because we find some type of enjoyment or pleasure in it. For example, in Isaiah 55:12, the prophet writes about the mountains and the hills bursting forth with song, and the trees of the field clapping their hands. Here we see a wonderful picture of a creation that is enjoying, singing about, and admiring its Creator. So there is a beautiful relationship that emerges. On the one hand we see that God enjoys His creation, and on the other hand we see that creation enjoys its Maker. I cannot explain all the intricacies of this remarkable relationship but Scripture certainly confirms that it exists.

Lastly but very importantly, we need to acknowledge that God delights in His creation because it brings delight to His people, and by doing this it points us to Himself. In Psalm 111:2 we read:

*"Great are the works of the Lord. They are pondered by all who delight in them."*

There is great pleasure that we experience in creation on a regular basis, whether it is the taste of a savory dish, the sight of a beautiful sunset, or the sound of birds singing as the dawn arrives. God enjoys the fact that we too can enjoy His creation, and when we take time to stop our busy lives and consider the wonders of this world, we are without excuse in knowing that He exists. When we see the grandeur of a place like Mt. Kilimanjaro, the magnificence of a Crowned Eagle, or the beauty of a cheetah walking across the grassland, and knowing that the Author of our salvation is the Author of all these amazing things that we see, a very appropriate response is to express our delight by saying, "Jesus, you are Lord, and you are awesome."

In my own ponderings I have often marveled at the fact that millions of people worldwide celebrate, admire, and are drawn to the beauty of pristine wilderness. One might ask, "Why do such great numbers of people have such an irresistible attraction to wilderness, including those who do not acknowledge our Lord?" "Why do they take such delight in being in places unspoiled by man?" Here is an answer to consider. Like no other place there is a sense of closeness to the Creator Himself that can be found in wilderness. Even though many would not be willing to admit it, this is what people relish the most, being close to their Creator. Some of the most memorable experiences in my own life have taken place in the unspoiled places of creation, where I have felt the unmistakable presence of my Savior. As Jonathan Edwards reminds us so well, the enjoyment of creation leads us to the enjoyment of our Savior.

> "When we are delighted with flowery meadows and gentle breezes of wind, we may consider that we see only the emanations of the sweet benevolence of Jesus Christ. When we behold the fragrant rose and lily, we see His love and purity. So the green trees and fields, and singing of birds are the emanations of His infinite joy and benignity (kindness & graciousness). The easiness and naturalness of trees and vines are shadows of His beauty and loveliness. The crystal rivers and murmuring streams are the footsteps of His favor, grace, and beauty."[33]

Before I draw this chapter to a close, I want to bring our attention to one final passage highlighting the words of Jesus. In today's world we often marvel at the far simpler things that man creates, and give much less attention to the things God has created. We turn our heads to watch the shiny new Mercedes Benz, we pat ourselves on the back for sending a spaceship to Mars, or we build up our egos by throwing a party to celebrate the doctorate degree we just received. Not that celebrating any of these things is wrong, mind you, but I want to emphasize how often we seem to ignore, overlook, and take for granted the far more glorious things which surround us each day; creatures and living organisms which far outshine our own design, our own engineering, and our own creativity. In Matthew 6: 28-29 Jesus reveals what I am trying to point out.

*"And why do you worry about clothes? See how the lilies of the field grow. They do not labor or spin. Yet I tell you that not even Solomon in all his splendor was dressed like one of these."*

While this passage is often used to caution against the habit of worrying, there is another golden nugget of truth that we can extract. Jesus points us to the reality and grandeur of what is evident in creation. Choosing the lily, just one species of flower amongst millions, He puts humanity in its appropriate place and He reminds us that the adornments and jewelry of the wisest and richest person ever to walk the earth cannot be compared to the marvels of this one flower. At first glance this lily may seem to be rather simple, and there is remarkable beauty in its simplicity. But upon further investigation we all know that this lily is far more complex than our computer programs or the engine in our car. It has the breath of life within it, allowing this plant to grow forth from the soil. This one flower is dressed so beautifully that we bring it into our homes to decorate our tables. This one flower has so much information packed into its DNA that it can multiply and reproduce itself many times over, free of charge. It does not need a factory or assembly plant to put the pieces together. Its living design goes far beyond our limited understanding.

Jesus is so right and we are often so forgetful of this fact. We should care for creation because it is beautiful and valuable beyond measure. We should care for creation because God delights in the exceedingly good works of His hands, and we too find great delight in those works. We should care for creation because what our Lord has made far outshines anything made by man. Martin Luther once made a statement that rings true with the statement Jesus made about the lilies of the field:

> *"In the true nature of things, if we rightly consider, every green tree is far more glorious than if it were made of gold and silver....God writes the gospel, not in the Bible alone, but also on trees, and in the flowers and clouds and stars."* * *

* * Several references attribute this quote to Martin Luther but it does not have a known source in Luther's writing.

Principle 10

# We care for creation because God is the owner of all things

Earlier in this book we discussed the concept of exercising Christ-like dominion over creation, and we were reminded of the parable of the Tenants found in Matthew 21. This story recalls how the owner of a vineyard hired tenants to take proper care of what rightfully belonged to him. Instead of exercising their responsibilities these tenants became wicked, they showed great disrespect to the owner and they even conspired to seize the vineyard for themselves. Jesus told this parable to illustrate how mankind would commit the most blatant act of disrespect in human history. Christ, the son of God, was about to be rejected by humanity and nailed to the cross, and in all of human history we can think of no greater insult.

Let us keep this parable in the back of our minds as we now consider God's ownership of creation and how that should influence our perspective. There are several passages that we could examine, but Psalm 24:1 and Psalm 50:9-11 are good places to start.

*"The earth is the Lord's, and everything in it, all the world and all who live in it; for he founded it upon the seas and established it upon the waters."*

*"I have no need of a bull from your stall or of goats from your pens, for every animal of the forest is mine, and the cattle on a thousand hills. I know every bird in the mountains, and the creatures of the field are mine."*

These Scriptures are short but powerful. We saw earlier that God is the Creator and Sustainer of all things, but now the fullness of His sovereignty over creation is broadened even further when we appreciate that He is the owner of all things. While this comes as no surprise, we need to carefully absorb the significance of this truth. Not only does God own everything, but He also knows every detail about everything that He owns. He knows about *"every animal"* in the forest and *"every bird in the mountains."* It is one thing to own a mansion, and the many acres that surround it. It is quite another thing to know each and every detail about the mansion itself, not to mention all of the trees, flowers, insects and birds which live on the property. In God's case we learn that He owns all the mansions and properties of the world and all of the *"cattle on a thousand hills"*. With this extraordinary truth in hand we can be quite certain that God also knows about every instance when we might abuse a part of His creation. As Matthew 10:29 reminds us, His knowledge is so comprehensive that He is aware of every sparrow that falls to the ground.

There is a high standard to uphold when we are in possession of something that does not belong to us, an obligation to respect and care for something that is owned by another. We all agree that we should uphold this standard whether we borrow something from our friend, our neighbor, or a prominent leader in our country. In every case, an item we have borrowed should be returned to its owner in the same condition as when we borrowed it. Better yet, to express our appreciation, we may even take steps to repair or improve that item so that the owner can enjoy receiving it back in even better condition.

The point is simple but significant. If we are willing to uphold this kind of standard for the things that we borrow from our fellow human beings, how much more should we uphold an even higher standard for the things that belong to the God of the universe? Indeed, by the virtue of His all-surpassing excellence, our obligation is much greater.

When mankind nailed Christ to the cross this was indeed the most blatant act of disrespect in human history. What we must realize is that when we treat God's creation with contempt, we only add insult to injury. We care for creation because God is the owner of all things, and because our desire is to show our respect and admiration for everything which He has made.

101

Principle 11

# We care for creation because God desires that we bring mercy and justice to the poor

Several places in Scripture remind us of our Christian obligation to bring mercy and justice to the poor. Proverbs 21:13 provides prudent words of caution for those of us who are in a position to do something about it.

> "If a man shuts his ears to the cry of the poor, he too will cry out and not be answered."

Have we truly done our best in answering the cries of the poor? An honest soul-searching would reveal that many of us have failed in this regard. Too often we have paid little attention to these matters, much less than they deserve. When it is our turn to cry out for help we run the risk that those cries might go unanswered. As we consider the cry of the poor from an environmental perspective it would be useful to give some reflection to the following questions:

- What kind of people live in the most damaged and unhealthy parts of our world?

- When environmental degradation takes place who are the first victims that often end up facing the most serious consequences?

- What segment of society is least able to defend itself when environmental injustice occurs?

The answers are obvious. We all recognize it is often the impoverished, the uneducated, and those without a voice who are the first to be exploited for their minerals, their forests, or other natural resources. They are the ones who end up living in the most hazardous and polluted neighborhoods, who often have no choice but to eke out their existence on the least productive land, and who are most vulnerable to drought and shortages of food or water. Of course there are times when the reverse can be true. Disadvantaged or distressed people sometimes have no choice but to degrade the resources of creation for the sake of survival. Countless communities across the world, in both developed and underdeveloped nations, suffer hardships of many kinds because the creation mourns. We must recognize that the degradation of creation can often be a result of injustice.

One case I am familiar with comes from Ethiopia, a country I used to live in when I was a boy. Many farmers lived in fear during a period called the Derg, where an oppressive communist regime ruled during the 1970's and 1980's. Government officials were often allowed to seize land for themselves at will. A farmer who was a good steward, whose land was managed well, and whose crops appeared to be healthy and productive, was a farmer who risked losing his land altogether. A beautiful farm would stand out, drawing attention from greedy eyes. As a result many farmers allowed their land to deteriorate. After all, the ability to keep a piece of degraded land was better than no land at all. In any farming system the lack of justice and security inevitably cripples the progress that farmers might hope to make in the area of agricultural stewardship. The stranglehold of injustice brings suffering to both farmers and the creation that sustains them. This case in Ethiopia is just one of many examples in Africa where injustice has led to damaged landscapes.

Worldwide there are countless small-scale farmers who conduct their activities on land they would love to own but they cannot obtain a title deed. They work season after season with a great deal of uncertainty, not knowing if they will be able to remain on the land or if they will suddenly be evicted. Without the security of ownership that comes with a title deed even those who are committed to good stewardship will find it more difficult to spend the extra effort required to care properly for the land.

There are many forms of injustice that bring ruin to creation and which lead to the hardship and suffering of people. Reformed Church leader Wesley Granberg-Michaelson summed it up well when he said the following:

> *"Injustice has its roots in seizing and controlling part of creation for one's own selfish desires and thereby depriving others of creation's fruits, making them poor, dispossessed and oppressed."*[34]

The business-as-usual mentality across much of our world is often reckless. It conducts activities that exploit both the resources of creation and the poor without thought and without remorse. Christians however, know very well that we serve a God of justice who has a special heart for the poor. His word throughout Scripture provides vivid reminders of this fact. Some powerful examples include the following:

*"If you do away with the yolk of oppression...and if you spend yourselves in behalf of the hungry, and satisfy the needs of the oppressed, then your light will rise in the darkness, and your night will become like the noonday. The Lord will guide you always; he will satisfy your needs in a sun-scorched land and will strengthen your frame. You will be like a well-watered garden, like a spring whose waters never fail." (Isaiah 58: 9-11)*

*"He has showed you, O man, what is good. And what does the Lord require of you? To act justly and to love mercy and to walk humbly with your God." (Micah 6:8)*

While both of these passages offer valuable instruction, I want to give special attention to the words in Isaiah 58:9-11. Note the distinct calling to meet the needs of the oppressed, and how God decorates this remarkable admonition with various themes of creation, including light, land, and water.

When we obediently answer God's call to bring justice and mercy to the poor, He draws a stunning parallel to highlight the significance of this type of loving intervention. As we work to bless those who are oppressed, the value of that effort becomes as valuable as light in the darkness. This light not only offers spiritual benefits, but it also leads to physical blessing. In the minds of the poor and hungry their most pressing needs are normally physical in nature. In some cases their lives are at stake and they are unable to give attention to other matters of life until they have received the life-giving provisions from creation. When we work to meet the physical needs of such people the genuine love of Christ is demonstrated. This testimony then opens the door for the truth of Christ to enter a situation in desperate need of such truth. By spending time and energy on such issues our lives become just like *"a well-watered garden, like a spring whose waters never fail."* The beauty emerging here is that the blessings flow both ways, reminding us that our obedience to this call is a win-win situation for all parties involved. The hungry are blessed, and those who spend themselves on *"behalf of the hungry"* are also blessed.

As we rejoice in this wedding of blessings we should also note that many believers have not yet made this connection. One unfortunate view sometimes expressed by certain church leaders is the idea that we should not worry so much about environmental matters, but rather, we should focus our concern on moral issues, the plight of children, and family values. I actually heard these words uttered by a prominent and well-known Christian speaker over the radio.

At first glance there are many who might agree with this notion. However, a closer inspection reveals a false dichotomy. We need to realize that our relationship with creation is a moral issue, and unfortunately, countless families and children around the world are suffering today because we have not embraced it as a moral issue. If we stop and think carefully, nothing could be more beautiful, more family oriented, and more honoring to God than to work with the poor, to ensure that justice prevails on their behalf, to bring healing to their land and to bring dignity back into their lives. When we come alongside such people, equipping them to feed and sustain their own families, we have just been reminded that the light of Christ will shine through us. This is just one of many ways we can open our ears to the cry of the poor. When the land mourns and becomes impoverished the people mourn and become impoverished. Let us care for creation so that we might become a refreshing well-watered garden to such people.

Principle 12

# We care for creation because it is the good, pleasing, and perfect will of God

We can agree that caring for creation will enrich our efforts to bring mercy and justice to the poor, improving our ability to live out the spirit of the Great Commandment. These themes also tie in well with yet another guiding principle for Christian living. God calls us not only to obedience; He also encourages us to pursue, to discover, and to carry out His will in all aspects of our lives. Have we ever engaged in deliberate efforts to think about the topic of creation in this way? When a lake is no longer sustaining a local community because of overfishing, or when cattle can no longer thrive on the grassland because of overgrazing, do we ever stop to ponder the following question: "God, what is your will for our community in this situation?"

Many Christians go to great lengths to seek, to pray, and to confirm God's will in issues like choosing the right marriage partner, selecting which church to join, or deciding whether a new job opportunity is something we should explore. We bring these questions and uncertainties to the foot of the cross and ask God, "What decision should I make? Please direct my thoughts and help me understand what I should do. I want to know and do your will in this matter." Very few of us have gone through this type of pursuit to discover how God might want us to relate to His creation. But that is exactly what we should be doing.

As the Apostle Paul reminds us, our perspectives should be radically different compared to the patterns that we see in the world.

> "Do not conform any longer to the pattern of this world, but be transformed by the renewing of your mind. Then you will be able to test and approve what God's will is, his good pleasing and perfect will." (Romans 12:2)

If we were to evaluate ourselves as members of Christ's body, how would our perspective of creation match up with the world's way of thinking? Are we conformed primarily to the pattern of this world, or are we conformed primarily to a pattern defined and directed by God's word? Are we making substantial efforts in testing and approving what God's *"pleasing and perfect will"* might be when it comes to caring for the creation, or do we form our opinions and decisions based on the secular influences of politics, materialistic temptations, and the prevailing views of economics? If we are honest with ourselves we know what this evaluation reveals and where our answers to such questions would fall. Many of us within the Church have been viewing creation more through the eyes of the world than through the eyes of God. Fortunately we have some excellent examples from

Christians long ago who had a perspective of creation defined by truth and soaked in the word of God. When we read the following quote by Charles Spurgeon we observe a person who is truly looking at things through a biblical lens. He sees creation accurately, in the same way that God does.

> "Fruit trees and forest trees, trees deciduous or evergreen, are equally full of benevolent design, and alike subserve some purpose of love; therefore, for all and by all, let the Great Designer be praised. There are many species of cedar, but they all reveal the wisdom of their Maker. When kings fell them, that they may make beams for their palaces, they do but confess their obligation to the King of trees, and to the King of kings, whose trees they are. Varieties in the landscape are produced by the rising and falling of the soil, and by the many kinds of trees which adorn the land. Let all, and all alike, glorify their one Lord. When the trees clap their hands in the wind, or their leaves rustle in the gentle breath of Zephyr, they do to their best ability sing out unto the Lord."[35]

Notice how Spurgeon begins. The trees of the forest are wonderfully designed and have an ultimate purpose. They point us to God. But he also recognizes that the forest fulfills another purpose. Yes, it is acceptable to cut trees down to build structures and to provide for the needs that we might have. We are able to use what the land supplies for our benefit. But in the same sentence he gives a caution. We should never forget the King of kings who owns and who has provided those supplies. What emerges here is the fact that we must strike a careful balance in our relationship with creation. When we use the forests, the water, the fish, the animals and other such resources, we must always do so in a way that demonstrates and upholds a tremendous respect for those resources. As Spurgeon reminds us so eloquently, they too are meant to bring glory to God.

This quotation provides a wonderful example for Christians to follow, and it is unfortunate that more of us do not think in this way. The disposition that Spurgeon reflects in his words reveals a person not only conformed to the ways of God, but who would be inclined to the pursuit of God's will in matters pertaining to the environment. If we could honestly say that our worldview on this matter was conformed to the will of God, then we would have to answer some tough questions. Why is the topic of creation care such a rare theme to be addressed from our pulpits or in our Sunday school classes? Why don't more of our Bible colleges and seminaries offer thoughtful, well developed biblically-based courses on this subject? While some good Christian books have been published on the subject, why are they so few in number?

Ed Brown, the director of Care of Creation Inc., is committed to stimulating a much needed change based on the challenge given to us in Romans 12:2. He has posed a simple but comprehensive one-sentence prayer that captures the essence of how we should apply this passage. Christians worldwide need to begin a fervent pursuit of God's will by placing this kind of request at the feet of our Lord:

> "God, what is your will for us as your people living on this part of your creation?"

In a simple prayer like this we see the beauty of humility, we see a quest for guidance from above, and we see the recognition of biblical truth. A prayer of this nature acknowledges that conforming to the patterns of this world cannot solve the problems afflicting creation today. We need God's help on this one. So our hope is in God and in people whose hearts and minds have been conformed to the mind of God. If we are obedient and committed to carrying out His good, pleasing, and perfect will, transformation will take place. This kind of prayer is also the starting point for a God-centered vision. Surely the development and implementation of such a vision is part of God's will for us who live in His creation.

Principle 13

# We care for creation because Christ will redeem and restore all things

Some of the most beautiful moments in life take place when people are reconciled to one another. We rejoice when broken relationships are restored, when people who were divided from one another, or once claimed to hate each other, are brought together again. This is the essence of what Christ's work on the cross has done on our behalf, enabling much-needed healing to take place in our broken relationships with our brothers and sisters and with God. This kind of reconciliation is a deep and a meaningful part of our own human experience, but have we ever considered the broader plan of God, and the fact that He also intends to bring the same kind of healing and restoration to the brokenness we see in the rest of His creation?

Living in a variety of places both in Africa and North America has blessed me with the chance to rub shoulders with a wide variety of Christians from multiple denominations. One thing I have consistently noticed is that our concept of redemption is often a narrow one. Many believers hold a rather limited view of Christ's sacrifice, assuming that His death and resurrection only holds implications for the redemption of mankind. While that is certainly a very significant part of the picture, it is not the whole picture. There are important Scriptures that we should examine as we begin to consider what the whole picture really looks like.

> *"For God was pleased to have all his fullness dwell in him, and through him to reconcile to himself all things, whether things on earth or things in heaven, by making peace through his blood, shed on the cross."* (Colossians 1:19-20)

This passage is a clear reminder that Christ's work of reconciliation on the cross is a total, all-encompassing and complete work. It extends to the whole cosmos, which includes the entire world and universe that God has created. One day complete healing and peace will be brought to everything on earth and in heaven because of what Christ has done. This wonderful news is consistent with what we have already learned. Since Christ, through His power, was able to bring the whole of creation into existence, it makes sense that He also has the power to restore everything that has been damaged as a result of man's sin. Not only can He do this, He has a vested interest in doing so. As we learned earlier from Colossians 1, the ultimate purpose of creation is to stand as a testimony of Christ's beauty and glory. Since creation has a divine purpose for its existence we can understand that Christ also has a desire to restore that which He enjoyed creating in the first place.

There are other parts of scripture which also point to the fullness of Christ's work on the cross. When we go back to the Old Testament we catch the very first glimpse of this truth as seen in the account of Noah. Right there, at the beginning of Scripture, in chapters 6-9 of Genesis, we learn about a God whose heart is filled with pain because of man's sin, but He still longs to rescue and restore a peaceful relationship with both mankind and the rest of His creation. God gives Noah very explicit instructions to preserve many kinds of animals, and His concern for all creation is reinforced through His covenant that is highlighted towards the end of the story in chapter 9:13-15.

> "I have set my rainbow in the clouds, and it will be a sign of the covenant between me and the earth. Whenever I bring clouds over the earth and the rainbow appears in the clouds, I will remember my covenant between me and you and all living creatures of every kind."

This preview from the Old Testament becomes more brilliantly portrayed when we move on to Romans 8. Here we read a gripping account that highlights how both mankind and creation long for the redemption that Christ is going to bring.

> "I consider that our present sufferings are not worth comparing with the glory that will be revealed to us. The creation waits in eager expectation for the sons of God to be revealed. For the creation was subjected to frustration, not by its own choice, but by the will of the one who subjected it, in hope that the creation itself will be liberated from its bondage to decay and brought into the glorious freedom of the children of God. We know that the whole creation has been groaning as in the pains of childbirth right up to the present time.

*Not only so, but we ourselves, who have the first fruits of the Spirit, groan inwardly as we wait eagerly for our adoption as sons, the redemption of our bodies."*
*(Romans 8:18-23)*

As Dr. John Piper once summarized so well, there is great hope for God's children and for creation in this passage. First, God wants us to see His promise that this time of suffering is temporary. It is going to come to an end, and afterwards we will see and experience a greatness and beauty beyond our wildest dreams. Secondly, He promises that the children of God will be revealed. One day we will truly become like the people we were meant to be. The creation waits eagerly for such people. Thirdly, God reveals that even in the midst of this suffering there is hope. The pain experienced today is not the pain of death, it is only labor pain. One day the entire creation will be liberated from its bondage to decay and something new will be born. Our bodies will be redeemed, creation will be redeemed, and the groaning of this world will pass away.

How does such wonderful truth affect our behavior today? The conclusion is both simple and profound. We live in a broken world, filled with pain, yet serve a God who calls us to be channels of His light and grace, a God who has a plan to redeem and restore His entire creation. If this is His plan, and if we confess to be His followers, then we should embrace His plan and follow in His footsteps. This demonstrates the healing power of Christ in the here and now, as we await His return, and it gladly looks forward to what God has purposed to accomplish in the future. We should be working to redeem and restore as much brokenness as we can, including the brokenness we see in creation.

Let us now turn our attention to the closing pages of Scripture, and the picture that it paints regarding our eternal home and the paradise that we will one day enjoy with Christ.

Principle 14

# We care for creation because we want to point people to our eternal home and paradise with Christ

One thing is true for all people of all nations. After facing the hardships of a broken world, the stress of a difficult week at work, or other frustrations in life, we all long to go home. While many in our world may not find pleasant circumstances in their respective homes, we all know that in its truest sense, home should be a place of rest, acceptance, love, fellowship, and comfort. We long for home because it is our place of refreshment. What is extraordinary about the gospel is that Christ clearly communicated that He came to earth so that He might bring His people home. And indeed it will be a wonderful home. John 14:1-3 records the wonderful promise that Jesus made to His disciples.

> *"Do not let your hearts be troubled. Trust in God; trust also in me. In my Father's house are many rooms; if it were not so, I would have told you. I am going there to prepare a place for you. And if I go and prepare a place for you, I will come back and take you to be with me that you may also be where I am. You know the way to the place where I am going."*

For those who embrace Christ as Lord this passage certainly raises a sense of wonder and curiosity about our future home. What does the home of our heavenly Father look like? What kind of place will this be? We can begin to get some answers to these questions when we read II Peter 3:13 and the last two chapters in the book of Revelation.

*"But in keeping with his promise we are looking forward to a new heaven and a new earth, the home of righteousness." (II Peter 3:13)*

*"Then I saw a new heaven and a new earth...I saw the Holy City, the new Jerusalem, coming down out of heaven from God, prepared as a bride beautifully dressed for her husband. And I heard a loud voice from the throne saying, 'Now the dwelling of God is with men, and he will live with them. They will be his people, and God himself will be their God. He will wipe away every tear from their eyes. There will be no more death or mourning or crying or pain, for the old order of things has passed away.' " (Revelation 21:1-4)*

*"Then the angel showed me the river of the water of life, as clear as crystal, flowing from the throne of God and of the Lamb down the middle of the great street of the city. On each side of the river stood the tree of life, bearing twelve crops of fruit, yielding its fruit every month. And the leaves of the tree are for the healing of the nations." (Revelation 22:1-2)*

Here at the end of Scripture, when we combine John 14 together with II Peter 3 and Revelation 21 and 22, we begin to capture a magnificent picture of our future home. From

Adam and Eve and the Garden of Eden, to the Promised Land flowing with milk and honey, the story now comes full circle when we read about the new heaven and new earth. This is going to be a place beyond our wildest imagination. This place will be a home of righteousness with no evil, no pain, no suffering, and no hunger. This new heaven and new earth is a dwelling where we will enjoy the very presence of God Himself. The *"river of the water of life"* is clean and pure beyond all measure, and it is a prominent feature flowing directly out of the throne of God and down the streets of the New Jerusalem. The tree of life is a prominent feature as well, and it will be so productive that it will usher forth a new crop of fruit every month. The intense pleasure of eternal fellowship with our Creator will be enjoyed in the most fitting of contexts. We will be there with Him, and we will be surrounded by and drenched in the splendor of His new creation. This describes the kind of place that all peoples of the earth have always longed for.

Given this glorious picture we must pause and ask ourselves some important questions. If this is the future we can look forward to, what is the point of today's feverish pursuit to accumulate and consume as many earthly treasures as possible? What more could money buy, or what more could the things of this world add to our eternal home? While we can easily accept the caution to not be swept into the idolatry of materialism, this gives us cause to ask yet another question. How does this hope for the future motivate us to care for creation today?

Unfortunately there are many Christians who harbor an escapist mentality that is reflected by a chorus we often sing in church:

*"This world is not my home, I'm just a-passing through. My treasures are laid up somewhere beyond the blue..."* This kind of thinking leads to the following conclusion: If I'm just passing through and will escape this world filled with suffering, why should I care about the environment? I'm heaven bound. If everything is going to be renewed and restored later why should we bother trying to fix things now? Unfortunately, as the previous chapters of this book demonstrate, this is a shallow, dangerous, and ungodly worldview. It is a mindset that needs to be corrected. Let me provide that correction by using a simple illustration.

Imagine that a Christian husband and wife are blessed with a daughter who has recently started school. She has made friends, is excelling in her ability to learn, and one day her life is tragically altered. A visit to the doctor reveals a rare and lethal form of cancer. The little girl only has a few months of life remaining. Now suppose that one morning, as the family wakes up, the husband turns quietly to his wife and states the unthinkable: *"We don't need to feed our daughter or take her to school anymore because she is going to die anyway. We're just passing through a tough time in life, and the sooner it's over the better."* In complete shock the mother to this child stares at her husband in disbelief. Speechless for a moment she then marshals a furious response to express her intense outrage. How could her husband utter such horrifying words?

Without question we would all agree wholeheartedly with the mother. In the same way we also know what the appropriate and God-glorifying course of action would be in a situation like this. The husband and wife would go to their knees in prayer each and every day. They would request God for help, they would plead with God for healing, and they would fervently do anything and everything within their power to love and minimize the suffering for their little girl. Christians need a similar response when it comes to a groaning creation. We need to glorify God, to the best of our ability, in a difficult and often daunting situation. Ignoring the crisis or failing to care for creation only sends a horrifying message to others, much like the one expressed by this husband. Both current and future generations deserve a thoughtful and hopeful response from the Church that encourages people everywhere to get involved in praying each and every day, a Church that encourages them to do everything that God would want them to do. We must point people to the glorious figure of Christ, for whom and through whom all things were made.

The truth that Christ is going to restore all things in the end does not in any way diminish our responsibility to care for creation in the here and now. In fact, the opposite is true. Christ's future work on our behalf should serve as a catalyst and springboard that adds fuel to the fire. It provides even greater incentive and motivation to do what is right. It should build within us a sense of determination and resolve to energetically bring about much needed change. This kind of response honors Him and affirms all the other principles that have been presented so far.

When we care for creation we bring glory to God, we enhance our testimony for Christ, we extend love to other people, and we point them to the future paradise that is in store for us.

We must therefore redouble our efforts to share the gospel, in as many ways as possible, so that those who have not yet embraced Christ as Lord might have their names written in the Book of Life. We certainly don't want anyone to suffer the wrath of God's judgment and neither do we want them to miss the opportunity to enjoy this paradise with Christ, with its endless wonders, its abundance, and all of its sights, sounds and colors. The matchless beauty of our future home, therefore, provides a most compelling reason why we should actively care for creation today.

# Final Thoughts

Of all people on earth, Christians have absolutely the best reasons to become actively involved in caring for creation, and absolutely the best news for a world that leaves God out of the picture as it strives to wrestle with this problem in its own strength. Humanity's attempt to address the issues at hand will be feeble and inadequate until we humble ourselves at the foot of the cross, confess our sin, and invite God to help. As Jesus once said to his disciples in Matthew 19:26: *"With man this is impossible, but with God all things are possible."*

As environmental concerns gain more attention on the world stage we have a truly wonderful opportunity to step forward and set the example, to provide God-centered leadership in a cause that longed for our engagement decades ago.

The cornerstone of our worldview on creation rests on the truth that Christ is the Creator of all things. Our primary motivation to care for creation flows from the basic but wonderful fact that we love the Creator. Our Lord and Savior, through His work on the cross, is moving history in a direction where He will one day redeem and restore all things. In keeping with His plan we need to follow in His footsteps by doing whatever we can to bring healing to creation.

We have understood the truth that God delights in His creation, just like we do, and that it has a primary purpose for its existence. The creation exists to serve as a testimony to the incomparable magnificence of the Creator. Apart from the Scriptures there is nothing else in this world that proclaims such a consistent and enduring message of God's reality and glory.

We are reminded that God Himself cares for the creation, and we are encouraged to consider carefully the difference between a worldly approach to dominion, characterized by greed and materialism, and pursue a radically different approach to our dominion, one that reflects the servant leadership and spirit of Christ.

In all these things we have ultimately recognized how caring for creation fits into our primary purpose in life, to glorify God in all things, and to demonstrate the immeasurable goodness of God in every aspect of what we think, say, and do. As we work to bring mercy and justice to the poor, as we show compassion to those who suffer from the effects of environmental decline, and as we make the necessary changes in our own lifestyles, we fulfill the Great Commandment. And as we holistically combine our work to fulfill the Great Commission with legitimate efforts to care for creation, our testimony for Christ will shine more brightly. Indeed what emerges here is a beautiful realization that all of this is in step with God's good, pleasing and perfect will for our lives.

Lastly, and of utmost importance, is the role that Christ can play in this world filled with sinners, and in a creation that groans because of that sin. Since He is the One who has created the wonders of this world, and since He is the One who performed the ultimate act of love by dying on the cross for our sin, and since He is the One who can radically transform the lives of those who accept Him as Lord, then He is also the One who can give us victory over the sins which destroy creation. This is where our most promising hope lies. The search for a solution to this crisis and to all the problems of this world must begin at the foot of the cross. It must be founded upon the life-changing and sin-conquering power of an active and maturing relationship with Jesus Christ. Christians need to bring Christ to those who have not yet experienced His saving grace, and we need to demonstrate how Christ has transformed our own lives. Our witness should be so appealing that it will draw others to join us in worshipping the Lord of all creation.

Please join me in using these principles to usher in a much needed change in the worldwide body of Christ. The creation is beautiful and valuable beyond measure because it points us to the Creator, the Alpha and the Omega, the Beginning and the End. As the representation of Christ's body we need to excel in our ability to preach powerfully on this topic, to develop effective Bible studies, Sunday school lessons, college courses for our young people and seminary courses for church leaders that all reflect a biblical worldview. We need to examine this issue more carefully through God's eyes, and design worship music, educational materials, mission strategies, and many other practical means that demonstrate our commitment to bring healing to a broken world. This commitment should also clearly demonstrate our desire to bring people hope for eternity and hope for today. In all these things our response should reflect that God is at the very center of our perspective and behavior as we relate to His creation.

# Appendix 1
# About Care of Creation Kenya

Care of Creation Kenya (CCK) is an evangelical mission organization dedicated to awakening churches, leaders and communities to their responsibility in creation care and environmental stewardship. We cherish the truth that Christ is our hope for eternity. We also believe that Christians should work to bring people hope for today by healing and restoring the landscapes of Kenya. CCK is a registered Company Limited by Guarantee under The Companies ACT of the laws of Kenya.

## Our Mission statement

Our mission is to pursue a God-centered response to the environmental crisis in Africa which brings glory to the Creator, advances the cause of Christ, and leads to a transformation of the people and the land that sustains them.

## Our Core Values

1) The truth of God's Word and the power it holds to transform the lives of people.

2) The Lordship of Christ over all creation and over all aspects of life.

3) Obedience to and the fulfillment of the Great Commission and the Great Commandment.

4) God-centered environmental stewardship (the nurture, promotion, and practical implementation of a God-centered perspective and concern for all of His creation).

5) Holistic ministry (the healing and restoration of man's relationship to God, humanity, and the rest of creation; a ministry to the whole person, both spiritually and physically).

6) Exemplary and Christ-like concern for and treatment of people.

## What We Do

Promoting a God Centered Vision
- Spreading a biblical vision for creation-care by training leaders, churches, communities and institutions through local and national conferences and workshops.

- Developing and distributing biblically-based books and educational resources on creation-care.

- Mentoring and certifying quality trainers who can effectively spread a vision for creation care and agricultural stewardship.

- Partnering with churches and other organizations working to address the environmental issues of Africa.

Promoting God-centered Action
- Farming God's Way
  - Equipping community leaders and farmers to implement a vision for restoring agricultural landscapes through a biblically-based approach to conservation agriculture.

- Tree Planting and Forest Conservation
  - Advancing the development of a tree-planting culture to restore our forests, protect biodiversity, and improve livelihoods.

- Training in other creation-care issues
  - Biblical principles of creation-care
  - Benefits and use of fireless cookers
  - Tree nursery management and grafting of fruit trees
  - Beekeeping

## Books and resources available at the Care of Creation Kenya office

Creation care books
- Honoring Christ in Caring for His Creation (by Craig Sorley)

- Farming that Brings Glory to God and Hope to the Hungry (by Craig Sorley)

- Let's Restore our Land (by Dr. Dan Fountain)

- Our Father's World (by Edward R. Brown)

- When Heaven and Nature sing (by Edward R. Brown)

- Creation Care and the Gospel: Rethinking the Mission of the Church (Edited by Colin Bell and Robert S. White)

Farming God's Way resources
- Farming God's Way Field Guide (by Grant Dryden)

- Farming God's Way Trainer's Reference Guide (by Grant Dryden)

- Farming God's Way Vegetable Guide (by Grant Dryden)

- Farming God's Way DVD Training Series (by Grant Dryden)

Other Resources
- Good Tree Nursery Practices (by ICRAF)

- Useful Trees and Shrubs for Kenya (by the World Agroforestry Centre)

- Restoring the Soil (by Roland Bunch)

- A Beginner's Guide to Beekeeping in Kenya (by Thomas Carroll)

## Contact information

Craig Sorley, Director
Care of Creation Kenya
c/o Moffat Bible College
P.O. Box 70 – 00220
Kijabe, Kenya

Office: (254) 731-772203
        (254) 712-772203
Mobile:(254) 733-451372
Email:  craig@careofcreation.org
Web:    www.careofcreationkenya.org

Care of Creation Inc. (USA)
P.O. Box 44582
Madison, WI 53744, USA
(+1) 608-233-7048
info@careofcreation.org
www.careofcreation.net

# Appendix 2

# Care of Creation Kenya Trainer Accreditation Program

*Transforming and Multiplying Quality Trainers for the glory of God and for the sake of those in need*

## Purpose of accreditation

The purpose of CCK's accreditation program is to multiply the number of highly qualified Christian trainers who have a comprehensive biblical worldview and vision for creation care. It is designed to equip candidates with a set of skills that qualifies them as a well-rounded creation-care trainer. Individuals are coached, mentored and evaluated, as required, depending on the gifts and capabilities they already possess.

## Summary of the accreditation process

A candidate entering the accreditation program engages in a process of hearing, reading, writing, implementing, and eventually speaking about a biblical worldview of creation-care. Various assignments and assessment tools are used to monitor and encourage a candidate's progress in the steps outlined as follows:

a) Hear and learn about the vision by attending one or more CCK trainings.

b) Read and write about the vision by engaging in a self-study process of creation-care books and Scripture.

c) Practically apply the vision by implementing creation-care solutions like tree-planting, Farming God's Way, etc.

d) Demonstrate your commitment to spread the vision by training others.

e) Conduct a formal training where your teaching capabilities can be assessed by other accredited trainers.

## Key outcomes and objectives

- Ensure that creation-care trainings are Christ-centered and biblically robust, communicating and displaying the fullness of the gospel.

- Demonstrate how creation-care trainings can complement and strengthen efforts in Christian ministry, including evangelism, discipleship, and reaching the unreached.

- Maximize the potential for both spiritual transformation of the inner person and physical transformation of landscapes.

- Maximize the potential to spread this vision more quickly across Africa, strengthening the effectiveness and practical impact of Christian leaders and of the Church.

- Maximize the impacts this vision can have upon the poor and upon future generations.

**Sequence of accreditation topics**

Track 1: Biblical Worldview for a Creation that Groans

Track 2: Farming God's Way

Track 3: Forestry and the Stewardship of God's Creation

For more details regarding CCK's accreditation program please submit your inquiry through the contact information provided in Appendix 1.

# Appendix 3

# Farming God's Way

*Discipling farmers to put God back into the center
of agriculture and more food on their tables*

*(a summary by Craig Sorley)*

*"Now the Lord God had planted a garden in the east
in Eden; and there he put the man he had formed.
And the Lord made all kinds of trees grow out of the
ground – trees that were pleasing to the eye and good
for food." Genesis 2:8-9*

## The Agricultural Crisis in Africa

What is the nature of agriculture in Africa today? In most
countries the majority of the population is comprised
of small scale farmers who depend upon rainfall and
hand-held tools to produce food for their families. The
unfortunate reality is that these farming communities have
experienced steady declines in per hectare food production
across much of the continent. Deforestation, soil erosion,
and other forms of land degradation have been the primary
culprits. In addition farmers are facing more frequent
droughts and increasingly erratic rainfall patterns. This is

a sobering reality in a world of rising population, rising food costs and the obvious need to increase crop yields on soils which already suffer from poor health.

While the description above presents a major challenge by itself, it is critical that we look even deeper to examine the social implications of this crisis. Only then can we appreciate the gravity of the situation. The physical "poverty" resulting from a decline in crop yields is accompanied by an equally if not more serious problem. A "poverty of spirit" is taking root in our communities. Farmers are discouraged, they are experiencing a greater sense of despair and hopelessness, and they lack the necessary vision for restoring their land. Unfortunately this "poverty of spirit" is being passed on to the next generation. Young people across many countries are rejecting farming as a viable vocation, viewing it as a non-profitable livelihood, and this holds serious implications for the future of small scale agriculture in Africa.

## Farming God's Way Offers a Viable Solution

Is there a solution that can turn this situation around both physically and spiritually? The answer is yes! The good news is that an encouraging movement is now sweeping across Africa called "Farming God's Way." It has a proven track record to both heal degraded land and improve crop productivity at the same time. In many cases three to five fold increases in crop yields have been realized.

## The Biblical and Spiritual Roots of Farming God's Way

The real beauty of Farming Gods Way is that it is much more than just a new system of growing crops. It is a training program that stimulates farmers to capture a vision for restoring their land and their soils. For the millions of farmers across Africa who embrace Christ as Lord, Farming God's Way is an attempt to put God back where He belongs - into the very center of how we view and practice agriculture. It is a holistic approach that ministers to farmers, addressing both the spiritual and physical roots of the declines that are taking place.

For Christians the story of agriculture begins in Eden, with the knowledge that God was the one who planted a magnificent and diverse garden (Gen 2:8-9). God was the First Farmer and He commissioned mankind (Adam and Eve) to work and take care of His garden (Gen 2:15).

This story brings tremendous meaning and dignity to the realm of agriculture. Farming is not merely a means of growing food, but it was meant to be a noble vocation of significant responsibility. Christian farmers need to follow the example of the First Farmer and uphold the Garden of Eden as a model to be pursued. Since Christ encouraged us to be perfect, as our heavenly father is perfect (Matt 5:48), we should strive towards perfection in the effort to become excellent stewards of the land.

But that is not all. There are many principles to be found in Scripture that clearly encourage us in this direction. Deuteronomy 11 provides one such example. After Scripture describes the "promised land" as a place *"flowing with milk and honey....a land of mountains and valleys that drinks rain from heaven"* (vs 9 and 11), we see the remarkable statement that God cared deeply about this place. Verse 12 reads: *"It is a land the Lord your God cares for; the eyes of the Lord your God are continually on it from the beginning of the year to its end."*

If the God we serve cares for the land *"from the beginning of the year to its end"* then what are the implications for us? By all means we should be following his example in doing the very same thing. These concepts from the Bible, following the example of the First Farmer, upholding the Garden of Eden as a model to be pursued, and caring for the land from the beginning of the year to its end are the transforming ideas that lie at the core of what is meant by "Farming God's Way".

## A Definition of Farming God's Way

When we start using a three-word phrase describing a movement that is beginning to sweep across Africa it is essential that we accurately communicate what this phrase really means, because it is a phrase filled with meaning. Since the Great Commandment is a very central concept to our Christian faith (loving God and loving our neighbor as ourselves) I would offer the following as a definition of what is ultimately meant by "Farming God's Way". Others may develop different or better versions of this particular definition.

> *Farming God's Way is the deliberate effort to bring God back into the center of how we view and practice agriculture, as a means of demonstrating our love for God and for people of both current and future generations. It seeks to blend a strong biblical and moral commitment for agricultural stewardship*

*with practices on the ground that bring restoration and healing to the land, resulting in improved crop productivity for the sake of the hungry and for the glory of God.*

*Farming God's Way recognizes that how we do agriculture should be an act of worship that reflects our devotion to the Creator and our desire to bring hope to the poor.*

## Farming God's Way Changes People and Farms

The bottom line is that when we allow God to enter our picture of agriculture He changes hearts, and when hearts are changed behaviors change. The tremendous potential of Farming God's Way lies in the fact that it does not separate the spiritual from the physical. Instead, it combines the two into one cohesive whole. Discipleship training, with sound biblical principles highlighting our moral obligation to be excellent stewards of the land, is combined with practical field techniques that redeem the land, bringing hope back into the lives of farmers. A spiritual conviction and a spiritual commitment, not handouts of seed and fertilizer, becomes the driving force for change. As farmers work to implement practices that restore their land, they realize that their faithful efforts to honor God are also bringing more food into the home.

## Summarizing the Practical On-The-Ground Technique

Farming God's Way is essentially a biblically-based version of a system known as Conservation Agriculture. The process begins with planting a God-given commitment into the hearts of farmers, with the basic goal of teaching farmers how to rebuild the overall health, fertility, and water-holding capacity of their soils. This leads to increased crop yields that can be sustained over time. Some of the key elements of this system include:

- **Zero tillage / no plowing:** The practice of plowing destroys soil structure and fertility as well as organisms that live in the soil, leading to erosion and rapid evaporation of water.

- **Cover the land at all times with God's blanket (a layer of mulch):** In creation we observe that God does not leave the soil bare. He covers the soil with protective vegetation or mulch (like grass covering the soil in grassland areas or like fallen leaves covering the forest floor). This provides multiple benefits:
  - Stops soil erosion
  - Captures and traps rainfall improving the infiltration of water into the soil
  - Minimizes evaporation of water from the soil, helping to mitigate dry spells and even the effects of drought
  - Adds organic matter, improving the fertility & water holding capacity of the soi

- **No burning of crop residues:** These residues are kept on the land as food for the soil.

- **Weed faithfully:** Labor saved on plowing is transferred to a regular and consistent year-round habit of weeding.

- **Practice rotations with a diversity of crops:** God's garden was diverse.

- **Pursue high standards in all steps from A-Z and pay attention to detail:** Since we serve a God of high standards and detail we should give careful attention to everything on our farms throughout the whole year (including the proper spacing of plants, how fertilizer or manure is added, how seed is planted, how weeding is conducted, how mulch is maintained on the field, etc.). God is glorified when we strive for excellence.

- **Minimize waste in all things:** As stewards of what God has entrusted to our care, we strive to minimize the waste of time, money, seed, inputs, soil, water, organic matter, etc.

- **Incorporate trees as part of the system (agroforestry):** The idea of agroforestry is not man's invention. It is something that God demonstrated on the very first farm. His garden included many kinds of trees. Agroforestry involves the combination of agriculture and forestry with conservation practices for the purpose of long-term sustainability.

Farming God's Way is an effective discipleship-oriented ministry that works to redeem the land, uplift the plight of the poor, and advance the cause of Christ. It has tremendous potential to change the lives of millions, to fight drought, and to reverse the specter of hunger threatening communities across Africa. In the past several years of my

141

own experience I have clearly witnessed that when properly implemented, Farming God's Way really works. I would encourage everyone to learn more about this ministry and find ways to promote this effort in your own locality.

## The 10 Commitments of Farming God's Way

1) I commit myself to honor God as the First Farmer and to glorify Him in everything I do on the farm. I invite Him to become a central part of how I think about agriculture and how I practice agriculture.

*"And we pray this in order that you may live a life worthy of the Lord and may please him in every way: bearing fruit in every good work, growing in the knowledge of God..."*

*(Colossians 1:10)*

2) Upholding the Garden of Eden as my example, I commit myself to a process of restoration that makes my garden more and more like God's garden.

3) I commit myself to learning, applying, and communicating the biblical principles of what it means to be a Godly farmer.

4) I commit myself to learning, applying, and communicating the technical information of FGW that will bring healing to the land that God has entrusted to my care.

5) I commit myself to the pursuit of excellence in how

I manage my land by doing things on time, pursuing the highest standards, and minimizing the waste of resources.

6) I commit myself to become a good steward by using the various resources and tools God has given me to the best of my ability, and to bring my tithes and offerings to God.

7) I commit myself to gladly disciple others in my community about FGW in order to break the yoke of poverty, hunger, oppression, and dependency.

*"If you spend yourselves in behalf of the hungry, and satisfy the needs of the oppressed...You will be like a well-watered garden, like a spring whose waters never fail."*
*Isaiah 58: 10-11*

8) I commit myself to redeem the vocation of agriculture by teaching the truth that farming is a meaningful and noble way of life because God was the First Farmer, and to plant this truth into the hearts of the next generation.

9) I commit myself to plant trees as part of my FGW system.

*"And the Lord God made all kinds of trees grow out of the ground – trees that were pleasing to the eye and good for food. In the middle of the garden was the tree of life..."*
*Genesis 2:9*

10) Since God is the Author of all creation I commit myself to learning about additional ways to care for what He has made in order to bring people hope for today and hope for the future (i.e. use of fireless cookers and fuel saving cook stoves, biogas, water-harvesting technologies, grafting of fruit trees, beekeeping, control of pollution and proper management of waste, wildlife conservation etc.).

*"All things were created by him and for him."*
*Colossians 1:16*

**Written by Craig Sorley,
Director, Care of Creation Kenya
www.careofcreationkenya.org**

**For more detailed information
about Farming God's Way see
www.farming-gods-way.org**

# Appendix 4
# Practical ways to care for creation

*God blessed us with His vast creation, with features grand in every nation. Majestic mountains, fields and streams, creatures beyond our wildest dreams. He blessed us with the power to choose how all these blessings we would use. This leaves us with the obligation to protect His world from exploitation.*

Genevieve Neumann

## God's creation cares for you all of the time

*"God is good, all of the time, and all of the time, God is good."* This short saying is a commonly repeated pronouncement used in thousands of churches across Kenya almost every Sunday. While it is very appropriate to remind ourselves about the righteousness of God, we must recognize that this statement holds significant implications for our own lives. If God is good all of the time his followers have a moral obligation to live up to the very same standards. Perhaps it is appropriate to alter this saying in order to emphasize the fullness of its meaning. I would offer the following phrase as a more complete and fitting pronouncement to help remind ourselves of God's calling upon our lives.

*"God is good, all of the time, and He has called us to be good, all of the time."*

In light of this book, and our mandate to care for creation, let us take a moment to consider the fullness of how God's good creation cares for us all of the time. If we can appreciate how God's blessings from His creation are continually flowing into our lives, this can motivate us to respond with gratitude. If God's creation is blessing us all of the time, our responsibility as good stewards is this: We should gladly care for His creation "all of the time", from the beginning of the year to its end, as we learned from Deuteronomy 11 in Principle 7.

## A list of ways in which God's creation cares for us, all of the time.

1) His creation provides a constant supply of sunshine (our most important source of energy).

2) His creation provides life-giving water from rainfall, oceans, lakes, rivers, streams, and wells, which sustain our bodies and regulate temperatures and climate.

3) His creation provides countless species of trees, plants, and crops which constantly absorb sunlight and $CO_2$, providing multiple blessings that include:
   - Food, fruit, nuts, and fodder for animals
   - Oxygen to breath
   - Wood, fiber, and raw materials that support industrial activity and allow us to build homes, make tools, furniture, clothing, etc.
   - Shelter and habitat for birds, insects, and animals

4) He has made marine plants and algae which constantly absorb sunlight and CO2, blessing us with much of the oxygen we breath and most of the food required to support marine life and fish.

5) He has made soil that provides a continual nutrient base for all plant growth.

6) He has made livestock, poultry, and a variety of animals which continually consume plants, helping to provide us with meat, milk, eggs, cheese, leather, etc.

7) He has made insects and bees by the billions which continually pollinate our crops for free, providing important ecosystem benefits, and serving as a food source for fish, birds, animals, etc.

8) He has made an infinite number of bacteria, fungi, and other unseen organisms that contribute to soil health and which constantly decompose and recycle our waste.

9) His creation provides multiple types of metal, stone, sand and other useful resources that allow us to create thousands of manufactured goods, tools, equipment, and appliances, which we use every day.

10) His creation provides a wide variety of precious jewels, minerals and chemicals used for important aesthetic, medical and industrial purposes

11) His creation provides oil, natural gas, and coal which enable many forms of transportation, the production of electricity, heat for our homes in the winter, etc.

12) His creation provides a dazzling array of creatures, mountains, valleys, stunning landscapes and starry heavens that display beauty beyond our comprehension and which brings refreshment to the soul.

## Practical creation-care activities for the African context

If God's creation cares for us all of the time, how much time and effort do we spend caring for His Creation? The list below outlines some ways in which we can exercise our commitment to be a good steward of all the blessings the Lord has provided. You may want to consider using this checklist as an evaluation tool for yourself, for members of your church, or in other educational settings.

## Check each creation care activity that applies:

- Preventing or minimizing erosion on my farm or in my community.

- Implementing sustainable agricultural practices, like Farming God's Way, to help conserve soil and water resources, and to minimize the waste of fertilizer, seed, time, etc.

- Planting trees.

- Caring properly for trees after planting by watering, weeding, pruning, and mulching them.

- Building up the diversity of plant life at home or on my farm by planting different kinds of crops, trees, flowers, etc.

- Collecting manure, compost, or mulch, and applying them to improve the health of my soil.

- Abstaining from the illegal cutting of trees or the use of charcoal and firewood which has been illegally harvested.

- Organizing, teaching, or promoting activities to stop destructive deforestation.

- Conserving energy from firewood or charcoal by using energy efficient cooking methods, or by using a Fireless Cooker.

- Using solar energy to produce electricity or installing a solar hot water heater in your home.

- Using LPG gas to cook food instead of using charcoal or firewood that leads to further deforestation.

- Installing and using a biogas system for cooking and lighting.

- Installing water harvesting systems to conserve water and using that water to improve the local environment (small dams, roof top water harvesting systems, etc.).

- Conserving and protecting birds and wildlife in my community by obeying and encouraging others to live in accordance with the laws about wildlife.

- Working or advocating against illegal poaching activity.

- Learning about the diversity of tree and wildlife species in my country (which species are rare or endangered, etc.).

- Studying about environmental issues or the biblical principles related to creation care.

- Developing bible-studies, Sunday school lessons, or teaching others about caring for God's creation.

- Preaching sermons about creation-care or encouraging your pastor to preach about this important topic.

- Exploring how your church can use creation care for missions and ministry purposes, to share the gospel with unreached people groups, to disciple existing believers, or to help needy people. This might include developing a formal creation care ministry as part of your missions or discipleship department.

- Planting trees and flowers around your church to make it as beautiful as possible and to glorify God.

- Inviting experts to your church or community to speak about creation care issues.

- Working to become an effective trainer in the biblical vision for creation care by studying the Scriptures, learning about Farming God's Way, reforestation, and other environmental topics.

- Actively communicating the importance of these issues to your community or government leaders.

- Disposing of waste and garbage properly.

- Working to pick up plastic bags and other forms of waste to make your community clean and tidy.

- Reducing garbage by recycling and reusing as many materials as possible (paper, glass, plastic bottles, metal cans, etc.).

- Identifying sources of pollution that damage air, soil, or water, and finding ways to stop or minimize that pollution.

- Using the power of the ballot to support community or government leaders who actively promote the stewardship and care of God's creation.

# Appendix 5

## The Cape Town commitment
### A Confession of Faith and a Call to Action
*©2011 The Lausanne Movement*

The concept of creation care was officially endorsed by thousands of evangelical leaders who attended the Third Lausanne Congress on World Evangelization held in Cape Town in October 2010. This appendix highlights the statements related to creation care which were published in the document entitled *"The Cape Town Commitment: A Confession of Faith and a Call to Action"* ©2011 The Lausanne Movement.

### Part I: Confession of Faith

### Item 7: We Love God's World
*Excerpts from pages 19-22 (I-7-A and I-7-E)*

We share God's passion for this world, loving all that God has made, rejoicing in God's providence and justice throughout his creation, proclaiming the good news to all creation and all nations, and longing for the day when the earth will be filled with the knowledge of the glory of God as the waters cover the sea.

A. We love the world of God's creation. This love is not mere sentimental affection for nature (which the Bible nowhere commands), still less is it pantheistic worship of nature (which the Bible expressly forbids). Rather it is the logical outworking of our love for God by caring for what belongs to him. 'The earth is the Lord's and everything in it.' The earth is the property of the God we claim to love and obey. We care for the earth, most simply, because it belongs to the one whom we call Lord.

The earth is created, sustained and redeemed by Christ. We cannot claim to love God while abusing what belongs to Christ by right of creation, redemption and inheritance. We care for the earth and responsibly use its abundant resources, not according the rationale of the secular world, but for the Lord's sake. If Jesus is Lord of all the earth, we cannot separate our relationship to Christ from how we act in relation to the earth. For to proclaim the gospel that says 'Jesus is Lord' is to proclaim the gospel that includes the earth, since Christ's Lordship is over all creation. Creation care is thus a gospel issue within the Lordship of Christ.

Such love for God's creation demands that we repent of our part in the destruction, waste and pollution of the earth's resources and our collusion in the toxic idolatry of consumerism. Instead, we commit ourselves to urgent and prophetic ecological responsibility. We support Christians whose particular missional calling is to environmental advocacy and action, as well as

153

those committed to godly fulfillment of the mandate to provide for human welfare and needs by exercising responsible dominion and stewardship. The Bible declares God's redemptive purpose for creation itself. Integral mission means discerning, proclaiming, and living out, the biblical truth that the gospel is God's good news, through the cross and resurrection of Jesus Christ, for individual persons, and for society, and for creation. All three are broken and suffering because of sin; all three are included in the redeeming love and mission of God; all three must be part of the comprehensive mission of God's people.

E. The World we do not love. The world of God's good creation has become the world of human and satanic rebellion against God. We are commanded not to love that world of sinful desire, greed, and human pride. We confess with sorrow that exactly those marks of worldliness so often disfigure our Christian presence and deny our gospel witness.

We commit ourselves afresh not to flirt with the fallen world and its transient passions, but to love the whole world as God loves it. So we love the world in holy longing for the redemption and renewal of all creation and all cultures in Christ, the ingathering of God's people from all nations to the ends of the earth, and the ending of all destruction, poverty, and enmity.

## Part IIB: Call to Action

### Item 6: Christ's Peace for His Suffering Creation
Excerpts from pages 46-47 (IIB-6)

Our biblical mandate in relation to God's creation is provided in the *The Cape Town Confession of Faith section 7(A)*. All human beings are to be stewards of the rich abundance of God's good creation. We are authorized to exercise godly dominion in using it for the sake of human welfare and needs, for example in farming, fishing, mining, energy generation, engineering, construction, trade, medicine. As we do so, we are also commanded to care for the earth and all its creatures, because the earth belongs to God, not to us. We do this for the sake of the Lord Jesus Christ who is the Creator, Owner, Sustainer, Redeemer and Heir of all creation.

We lament over the widespread abuse and destruction of the earth's resources, including its biodiversity. Probably the most serious and urgent challenge faced by the physical world now is the threat of climate change. This will disproportionately affect those in poorer countries, for it is there that climate extremes will be most severe and where there is little capability to adapt to them. World poverty and climate change need to be addressed together and with equal urgency.

We encourage Christians worldwide to:
    A. Adopt lifestyles that renounce habits of consumption that are destructive or polluting;

B. Exert legitimate means to persuade governments to put moral imperatives above political expediency on issues of environmental destruction and potential climate change;

C. Recognize and encourage the missional calling both of (i) Christians who engage in the proper use of the earth's resources for human needs and welfare through agriculture, industry and medicine, and (ii) Christians who engage in the protection and restoration of the earth's habitats and species through conservation and advocacy. Both share the same goal for both serve the same Creator, Provider and Redeemer.

# Appendix 6

# The Lausanne Global Consultation On Creation Care And The Gospel

## Call to Action

**St. Ann, Jamaica, November 2012**

### Introduction

The *Lausanne Global Consultation on Creation Care and the Gospel* met from 29 Oct – 2 Nov 2012 in St. Ann, Jamaica to build on the creation care components of the Cape Town Commitment. We were a gathering of theologians, church leaders, scientists and creation care practitioners, fifty-seven men and women from twenty-six countries from the Caribbean, Africa, Asia, Latin America, Oceania, North America and Europe. We met under the auspices of the Lausanne Movement in collaboration with the World Evangelical Alliance, hosted by a country and region of outstanding natural beauty, where we enjoyed, celebrated and reflected on the wonder of God's good creation. Many biblical passages, including reflections on Genesis 1 – 3, Psalm 8 and Romans 8, informed our prayers, discussions and deliberations on the themes of **God's World, God's Word and God's Work.** Our consultation immediately followed Hurricane Sandy's devastation of the Caribbean and coincided with that storm's arrival in North America; the destruction and loss of life was a startling reminder as to the urgency, timeliness and importance of this Consultation.

## Two major convictions

Our discussion, study and prayer together led us to two primary conclusions:

***Creation Care is indeed a "gospel issue within the lordship of Christ"*** (CTC I.7.A). Informed and inspired by our study of the scripture – the original intent, plan, and command to care for creation, the resurrection narratives and the profound truth that in Christ all things have been reconciled to God – we reaffirm that creation care is an issue that must be included in our response to the gospel, proclaiming and acting upon the good news of what God has done and will complete for the salvation of the world. This is not only biblically justified, but an integral part of our mission and an expression of our worship to God for his wonderful plan of redemption through Jesus Christ. Therefore, our ministry of reconciliation is a matter of great joy and hope and we would care for creation even if it were not in crisis.

***We are faced with a crisis that is pressing, urgent, and that must be resolved in our generation.*** Many of the world's poorest people, ecosystems, and species of flora and fauna are being devastated by violence against the environment in multiple ways, of which global climate change, deforestation, biodiversity loss, water stress, and pollution are but a part. We can no longer afford complacency and endless debate.

Love for God, our neighbors and the wider creation, as well as our passion for justice, compel us to "urgent and prophetic ecological responsibility" (CTC I.7.A).

## Our call to action

Based on these two convictions, we therefore call the whole church, in dependence on the Holy Spirit, to respond radically and faithfully to care for God's creation, demonstrating our belief and hope in the transforming power of Christ. We call on the Lausanne Movement, evangelical leaders, national evangelical organizations, and all local churches to respond urgently at the personal, community, national and international levels.

### Specifically, we call for:

1. **A new commitment to a simple lifestyle.** Recognizing that much of our crisis is due to billions of lives lived carelessly, we reaffirm the Lausanne commitment to simple lifestyle *(Lausanne Occasional Paper #20)*, and call on the global evangelical community to take steps, personally and collectively, to live within the proper boundaries of God's good gift in creation, to engage further in its restoration and conservation, and to equitably share its bounty with each other.

2. **New and robust theological work.** In particular, we need guidance in four areas:
   - An integrated theology of creation care that can engage seminaries, Bible colleges and others to equip pastors to disciple their congregations.

- A theology that examines humanity's identity as both embedded in creation and yet possessing a special role toward creation.

- A theology that challenges current prevailing economic ideologies in relation to our biblical stewardship of creation.

- A theology of hope in Christ and his Second Coming that properly informs and inspires creation care.

3. **Leadership from the church in the Global South.** As the Global South represents those most affected in the current ecological crisis, it possesses a particular need to speak up, engage issues of creation care, and act upon them. We the members of the Consultation further request that the church of the Global South exercise leadership among us, helping to set the agenda for the advance of the gospel and the care of creation.

4. **Mobilization of the whole church and engagement of all of society.** Mobilization must occur at the congregational level and include those who are often over-looked, utilizing the gifts of women, children, youth, and indigenous people as well as professionals and other resource people who possess experience and expertise. Engagement must be equally widespread, including formal, urgent and creative conversations with responsible leaders in government, business, civil society, and academia.

5. **Environmental missions among unreached people groups.** We participate in Lausanne's historic call to world evangelization, and believe that environmental issues represent one of the greatest opportunities to demonstrate the love of Christ and plant churches among unreached and unengaged people groups in our generation (CTC II.D.1.B). We encourage the church to promote "environmental missions" as a new category within mission work (akin in function to medical missions).

6. **Radical action to confront climate change.** Affirming the *Cape Town Commitment's* declaration of the "serious and urgent challenge of climate change" which will "disproportionately affect those in poorer countries", *(CTC II.B.6)*, we call for action in radically reducing greenhouse gas emissions and building resilient communities. We understand these actions to be an application of the command to deny ourselves, take up the cross and follow Christ.

7. **Sustainable principles in food production.** In gratitude to God who provides sustenance, and flowing from our conviction to become excellent stewards of creation, we urge the application of environmentally and generationally sustainable principles in agriculture (field crops and livestock, fisheries and all other forms of food production), with particular attention to the use of methodologies such as conservation agriculture.

8. **An economy that works in harmony with God's creation.** We call for an approach to economic well-being and development, energy production, natural resource management (including mining and forestry), water management and use, transportation, health care, rural and urban design and living, and personal and corporate consumption patterns that maintain the ecological integrity of creation.

9. **Local expressions of creation care, which preserve and enhance biodiversity.** We commend such projects, along with any action that might be characterized as the "small step" or the "symbolic act," to the worldwide church as ways to powerfully witness to Christ's Lordship over all creation.

10. **Prophetic advocacy and healing reconciliation.** We call for individual Christians and the church as a whole to prophetically "speak the truth to power" through advocacy and legal action so that public policies and private practice may change to better promote the care of creation and better support devastated communities and habitats. Additionally, we call the church to "speak the peace of Christ" into communities torn apart by environmental disputes, mobilizing those who are skilled at conflict resolution, and maintaining our own convictions with humility.

### Our call to prayer

Each of our calls to action rest on an even more urgent call to prayer, intentional and fervent, soberly aware that this is a spiritual struggle. Many of us must begin our praying with lamentation and repentance for our failure to care for creation, and for our failure to lead in transformation at a personal and corporate level. And then, having tasted of the grace and mercies of God in Christ Jesus and through the Holy Spirit, and with hope in the fullness of our redemption, we pray with confidence that the Triune God can and will heal our land and all who dwell in it, for the glory of his matchless name.

We, the participants of the 2012 Jamaica Creation Care Consultation, invite Christians and Christian organizations everywhere to signify your agreement with and commitment to this Call to Action by **signing this document** as an individual or on behalf of your organization, institution or other church body. Individuals may sign by going to http://www.lausanne.org/creationcare and following the directions given to add their names. Organizational signatories should send a letter or email signed by their leader, board chair, or authorized representative to creationcare@lausanne.org (Questions about this procedure may be sent to the same address.)

*Agreed together by the participants of the Lausanne Global Consultation on Creation Care and the Gospel, St. Ann, Jamaica, 9 November, 2012.*

**Call to Action Writing Team:**
Lowell Bliss (USA); Paul Cook (UK); Sara Kaweesa (Uganda); Lawrence Ko (Singapore).

## Consultation Senior Leaders:

Ed Brown, Sr. Associate for Creation Care; Las Newman, Lausanne Int. Deputy Director for the Caribbean; Ken Gnanakan, President, Int. Council for Higher Education. David Bookless, Advisor for Theology & Churches, A Rocha International.

## Consultation Participants:

Tyler Amy (US); Premamitra Anandaraja (India); Seth Ken Appiah Kubi (Ghana); Hoi Wen Au Yong (Singa¬pore); Tom Baker (UK); Frederic Baudin (France); Colin Bell (UK); David Bennett (US);; Samuel YuTo Chiu (Canada); Paul Cook (UK); Beth Doerr (US); Stan Doerr (US); Lindani Dube (Zim¬babwe); Darceuil Duncan (Trinidad and Tobago); Christopher Elisara (US); Susan Emmerich (US); Samuel Ewell (UK); Naomi Frizzell (US); David Gould (Singa¬pore); Peter Illyn (US); James Kalikwembe (Malawi); David Knight (Canada); Andrew Leake (Argentina); Terry LeBlanc (Canada); Jonathan Moo (US); Juliana Morillo (Peru); Osvaldo Munguia (Honduras); Cassien Ndikuriyo (Burundi); Claudio Oliver (Brazil); James Pender (Bangladesh); Mark Pierson (New Zealand); Lalbiakhlui Rokhum (India); Thomas Schirrmacher (Germany); Sally Shaw (Australia); Chris Shore (US); Mgliwe Simdinatome (Togo); Craig Sorley (Kenya); Joel Tembo Vwira (DRC); Efraim Tendero (Philippines); Denise Thompson (Trinidad and Tobago); Stephen Tollestrup (New Zealand); Ruth Valerio (United King¬dom); Peter Vander Meulen (US); Jean Valery Vital Herne (Haiti); Barry Wade (Jamaica); Serah Wambua (Kenya); Robert White (UK); Thomas Yaccino (US).

# End Notes

1. Martin Luther. *Sermons on the Gospel of John*. Ed. Jaroslav Pelikan. St. Louis: Concordia. 1957, 22:496.

2. Alina Bradford, 'Deforestation: Facts, Causes, & Effects', *Live Science*, 2015, accessed 18th May, 2016, http://www.livescience.com/27692-deforestation. html.

3. Alister Doyle, 'Africa's deforestation twice world rate, says atlas', *Reuters*, 2008, accessed 12th May, 2016, http://www.reuters.com/article/us-africa-environment-idUSL1064180420080610

4. National Environment Management Authority (NEMA). *State of Environment Report Kenya, 2003* (Nairobi: NEMA, 2004), 10.

5. 'Study: Kenya loses 5.6 million trees daily', *Africa Eco News*, 2015, accessed 14th April, 2016, http://www. capitalfm.co.ke/news/2015/03/study-kenya-loses-5-6-million-trees-daily/.

6. Ibid.

7. United Nations Environment Programme, *Kenya: Atlas of our Changing Environment* (Nairobi: UNEP, 2009), 10.

8. Roland Bunch, *Restoring the Soil* (Winnipeg, MB, Canada: Canadian Food Grains Bank, 2012), Preface.

9.   United Nations Environment Programme, *Kenya: Atlas of our Changing Environment* (Nairobi: UNEP, 2009), 74.

10.  United Nations Environment Programme, *Kenya: Atlas of our Changing Environment* (Nairobi: UNEP, 2009), 2.

11.  'Our Hot and Hungry Continent is Getting Hotter and Hungrier', *Daily Nation*, 2015, accessed 15th April, 2016, http://www.nation.co.ke/lifestyle/DN2/FOOD-SECURITY-Hotter-and-hungrier/-/957860/2857440/-/s93csu/-/index.html.

12.  Roland Bunch, *Restoring the Soil* (Winnipeg, MB, Canada: Canadian Food Grains Bank, 2012), 3.

13.  United Nations Environment Programme, *Kenya: Atlas of our Changing Environment* (Nairobi: UNEP, 2009), 106.

14.  Craig S. Sorley & D.E. Andersen, 'Raptor abundance in south-central Kenya in relation to land use patterns', *African Journal of Ecology* 32, no. (March 1994), 30-38.

15.  Vincent Ng'ethe, 'Report Warns on Big Wildlife Losses', *Daily Nation*, 3rd March, 2016, accessed 18th May, 2016, http://www.nation.co.ke/newsplex/Wildlifeday/-/2718262/3101744/-/c2sonx/-/index.html.

16. Sanskrity Sinha, 'Africa's dwindling lion population: Wildlife expert reveals why big cats are slowly dying in Kenya's Maasai Mara', *International Business Times*, 2016, accessed 12th May, 2016, http:// www.ibtimes.co.uk/africas-dwindling-lion-population-wildlife-expert-reveals-why-big-cats-are-slowly-dying-1542164.

17. 'Kenyan Lions on Brink of Extinction', *eNews Channel Africa*, 7 April, 2013, accessed 2nd May, 2016, https://www.enca.com/africa/lions-brink-farmer-retaliate.

18. Vincent Ng'ethe, 'Report Warns on Big Wildlife Losses', *Daily Nation*, 3rd March, 2016, accessed 18th May, 2016, http://www.nation.co.ke/newsplex/ Wildlifeday/-/2718262/3101744/-/c2sonx/-/index. html.

19. Helge Denker, 'Living with Wildlife: The Story of Namibia's Communal Conservancies', *Namibian Association of CBNRM Support Organisations*, 2011, accessed 12th May 2016, http://www.nacso. org.na/SOC_profiles/Namibia's%20Communal%20 Conservancies.pdf.

20. John Platt, 'Big News: Wild Tiger Populations are Increasing for the First Time in a Century', *Scientific American*, 2016, accessed 4th May 2016, http:// blogs.scientificamerican.com/extinction-countdown/ tiger-populations-increasing/.

21. Joseph A. Sittler, J. *Gravity and Grace: Reflections and Provocations*, (Minneapolis, MN: Augsburg. 1986), p. 15.

22. Ed Brown, *Our Father's World: Mobilizing the Church to Care for Creation*, (Downers Grove, IL: IVP, 2008), p. 43.

23. Edwards, Jonathan. *Observations Concerning the Scripture Oeconomy of the Trinity and the Covenant of Redemption*. New York: Charles Scribner's Sons, 1880.

24. Fagg, P. *Let Them Praise: Developing an Environmental Education Program that Honors the Creator,* Mancelona, MI: Au Sable Institute of Environmental Studies. 1998, p. 3.

25. John Piper, 'Love: The Labor of Christian Hedonism', *Desiring God online resources*, accessed 12th April, 2016, http://www.desiringgod.org/messages/love-the-labor-of-christian-hedonism.

26. Paul Brand, ' "A Handful of Mud": A Personal History of My Love for the Soil', in *Tending the Garden: Essays on the Gospel and the Earth*. ed. Wesley Granberg-Michaelson. (Grand Rapids, MI: William B. Eerdmans Publishing Co. 1987), p. 147.

27. Dan Fountain, *Let's Restore Our Land*, (Kijabe, Kenya: Today in Africa, 2007).

28. Lowel Bliss, *Environmental Missions: Planting Churches and Trees* (Pasadena CA: William Carey Library, 2013), 17.

29. Calvin, John. "Genesis 2:15 as Interpreted by John Calvin," *Commentaries on the First Book of Moses, Called Genesis*, translated from the original Latin (1554), and compared with the French edition, by John King, Vol. 1: Grand Rapids: Eerdmans, 1948, p. 125.

30. 'We scientists don't know how to do that', *Canadian Association for the Club of Rome*, 27th March, 2016, accessed 4th May, 2016, http://canadiancor.com/scientists-dont-know/.

31. Jaki, S. *Praying the Psalms: A Commentary*. Grand Rapids, MI: William B. Eerdmans Publishing Co. 2001, p. 49.

32. Piper, J. *The Pleasures of God*. Sisters, OR: Multinomah Publishers, Inc. 2000, p. 93.

33. Edwards, Jonathan. "The Excellency of Christ," *The Works of Jonathan Edwards Vol I*. Peabody: Hendrickson (2007) 680. Also available online at <http://www.ccel.org/ccel/edwards/sermons.excellency.html>

34. Granberg-Michaelson, Wesley. *A Worldy Spirituality: The Call to Take Care of the Earth*. San Francisco, CA: Harper & Row. 1984, p. 86.

35. Spurgeon, Charles. *The Treasury of David*. Vol VII. New York: Funk & Wagnals. 1886, p. 424.

## Notes to Appendix 5

1. The Third Lausanne Congress on World Evangelization, *The Cape Town Commitment: A Confession of Faith and a Call to Action* (Lausanne Movement, 2010; Hendrickson Publishers, 2011), I-7-A.

2. *Cape Town Commitment*, II-B-6-46.

## Notes to Appendix 6

1. Lausanne Movement, 'Lausanne Global Consultation on Creation Care and the Gospel: Call to Action' (St. Ann, Jamaica: Lausanne Movement, 2012).